"A Journey In God's Kingdom"

By

Bob & Gretchen Hyneckeal

Fujimo Publications

Reisterstown, Maryland

We want to hear from you about whether or not you enjoyed the book.
We value your suggestions, comments, and/or corrections.
Requests for information or to order copies, write to us at:

Bob and Gretchen Hyneckeal
117 Shetland Circle, Reisterstown, MD 21136
or
E-mail us at: fujimo4@juno.com

Cover design by Marketing Resources, Inc.
Interior design by Marketing Resources, Inc.

Library of Congress Control Number: pending
International Standard Book Number: **0-9771707-0-5**

First Printing: 500 copies

Robert Henry Hyneckeal graduated from Mt. St. Joseph High School in Baltimore, Maryland in 1962 and from the University of Notre Dame in South Bend, Indiana in 1967 with a five-year major in architecture and business.

Gretchen Fornoff Hyneckeal graduated from Western High School in Baltimore, Maryland in 1963, from Bradley University in Peoria, Illinois in 1967 with a BS Degree in Elementary Education, and from Rowan University (formerly Glassboro State College) in Glassboro, New Jersey in 1972 with a Master's Degree in Reading Education.

Table of Contents

"A Journey In God's Kingdom"

Bob and Gretchen Hyneckeal have long been dedicated friends and partners in the Habitat for Humanity ministry. Through their years of RVing, they have spent countless hours volunteering their time and enthusiasm to build homes with low-income families through this venture of hammering out God's love. Their dedication to helping others is truly inspiring and they are a blessing to all who know them.

Habitat for Humanity is a non-profit Christian housing organization that builds homes in partnership with families in need. Habitat homes are affordable to low-income families because they are built with volunteer labor and the families pay a mortgage at no-profit and no-interest. Volunteers make the Habitat system work and without people like Bob and Gretchen, Habitat would not exist! Both personally and as founder and president of Habitat for Humanity, I am so grateful for and to Bob and Gretchen.

This book is not only about Habitat, but is a diary of Bob and Gretchen's adventures across the U.S. The stories about working on Habitat builds, watching baseball games, and visiting national parks demonstrate how fulfilling a life on the road can be! It is my hope that you will read this book and not only enjoy the stories, but reflect on what you can do in your life to promote and advance God's Kingdom!

Millard Fuller
Founder and President
Habitat for Humanity International

"A Journey In God's Kingdom"

This book is dedicated

to the free spirit

within us all.

Acknowledgments

We thank Millard Fuller for his encouragement and support. We appreciate the Foreword he wrote for our book.

Bob's Aunt Esther was our inspiration for getting started. We are grateful to all of the friends who suggested we put into written words the stories we shared with them. There were also many others who contributed to our experiences that we drew upon to write this book.

We would like to especially mention the contributions of Marylou and Bob Benedict, Christen and Joshua Davenport, Abby Goward, Mary and Dave Lazor, Amy Nathan, and Joe Norkus. Their suggestions were invaluable.

Gretchen and Bob Hyneckeal

"Life is a journey, not a destination"

– Author Unknown

Introduction

This is not a book about what to do, how to do it, or what you should know. It's not a book about keeping track of mileages or directions or finding the best restaurants. It's simply a book about our full-time RVing experiences, our goals, our likes and dislikes. It is spattered with helpful hints. We're leaving out the parts about the particular relatives or friends we spent time with, unless we think there's an amusing story or something we thought might interest the reader. We're not museum enthusiasts and though we did visit some museums, the reader won't find that a focal point.

We traveled with a dog during most of our journey and tried to find suitable camping for him. We visited 46 of our nation's 55 national parks, 27 of the 30 major league baseball stadiums and 11 of the 12 presidential libraries. We participated in 10 Habitat for Humanity builds in various states. This information is documented in the appendices. We both felt that God had blessed us throughout our lives in so many ways that we liked the idea of being able to give back a little, a pass-it-on kind of thing. This and other miscellaneous adventures is what our book is about and we hope you'll enjoy it.

"The path to a peaceful life is so simple to travel,
yet many choose not to understand it."

— From *A Thousand Paths To A Peaceful Life* by David Baird

Chapter One

Introduction to The Full-Time RVing Lifestyle

A decision to travel

When Bob and I decided to give up our comfortable lifestyle to travel full time in a motor home, we can't remember. Not owning a motor home and not ever having traveled in that way before, we can only recall knowing that one of us suggested it and the other thought it sounded like a great idea. Neither of us had parents living and within the year our youngest child would have been going to college. In the past year before the suggestion was made, three of our dear friends had died before the age of 50. Bob had lost both of his parents in their 50s and my father had died at age 37. I think we were afraid we were going to miss out if we didn't do it soon. So far we had been tied to jobs during the week, lawn and housework on the weekends. Our six children at ages 29, 29, 27, 26, 21, and 17 at that time were all unmarried and all living on their own, supporting themselves except the youngest who soon would be. They led their own lives in various states, so leaving home would have given us more opportunity to visit with them.

Rob, our oldest by a week, had been adopted when he was two years old. Single and living in his own home, he was working as a fifth-grade teacher in Vineland, New Jersey. John, the same age as Rob, shared a townhouse with Arn, his younger brother, in Marlton, New Jersey. Also single, he worked in a job selling mortgages over the phone to already qualified clients. Arn, next in line, owned the townhouse that John shared with him. Single, he worked in the same field as John. Loren, a year younger than Arn, lived in Las Vegas, Nevada and shared a home with Brandi in an on and off relationship. Our granddaughter, Ashley had lived with her father and mother in Las Vegas as well as living with her mother alone in Spring Grove, Pennsylvania, and again with both her parents in Las Vegas. Loren drove heavy equipment for a living while Brandi drove a dump truck. They both enjoyed construction work. Robin, our only daughter lived in Union Bridge, Maryland and worked for the Police Department as a dispatcher. During our travels, she married Eric and they had a baby, our second granddaughter, Danielle. Joshua, our youngest attended school at Gordon College in Wenham, Massachusetts and married Christen near the end of our travels.

Buying a recreational vehicle (hereafter called RV or rig)

During the year that preceded our road trip, we attended some RV shows. We couldn't afford a new rig, but we wanted to see what options we might have. At the shows there were seminars about traveling, about whether or not we were suited for full-time RVing and about campground clubs and packages. If we joined a campground group, we could stay at campgrounds for discounted prices. We bought a campground package from a broker who sold packages previously owned by full-time RVers who had retired from the road. The package we bought included Coast to Coast and Resort Parks International (RPI). That allowed us to stay in one of the 600 campgrounds included in the package for five dollars per night. When we bought Coast to Coast and RPI in 1997, we had no idea that $350 was such a good deal. Many of the campground packages originally sold for thousands of dollars. We just knew that if we were going to be staying in a campground every night throughout the country that we would save a lot by spending $350 at that time. For six years we stayed in first-rate campgrounds for five and six dollars instead of the going rates from $15 to $35 per night. It turned out to be a huge savings. At this writing, in 2004, it still costs only six dollars per night to stay in a Coast to Coast Resort and there are hundreds of them all over the United States and Canada.

Bob had a business convention in Florida the spring before we left. He took a couple of extra days and I went along so that we could hunt for a used motor home. At the shows, there were so many RV options. We had decided on a motor home rather than a pull-behind trailer or a fifth-wheel trailer because a motor home seemed to be the easiest to setup once we got where we were going each night or each week. We were planning to move around quite a bit. We also liked the idea of being able to fix snacks and drinks while driving and not having to make pit stops. Of course we would have had to pull over when the driver needed one, but we wouldn't have to get out like you would in a trailer or fifth wheel. It would also be nicer to have our pets traveling comfortably with us. We liked the idea of having a car in tow to use for sightseeing when we got to a campground rather than driving in a pick-up truck. If we made friends in a campground we thought we could invite them to go out with us in our car. It would be so much easier to unhitch the car than to have to get a pick-up truck free of the trailer. If we should arrive in the rain, we wouldn't have to get out of the motor home until the rain stopped. In a trailer we would have had to get out to set up, raining or not. We also decided to use a tow bar rather than a dolly to pull the car. That turned out to be a wise choice, as many campground sites did not have extra space for storing a dolly.

We had been told that the most used RVs would be in Florida or Arizona, states where many folks settle after their RVing days are over. We traveled around Florida checking out dealers and newspaper ads. We quickly discovered that many options we had liked in the new RVs weren't necessarily available in used RVs. I decided I could do without a bathtub and Bob decided he could do without a backup camera if he had a back window. We wanted something sturdy and we didn't want to spend more than $35,000. Whatever we had left from the sale of the house would be what we would have to live on. Our dream was to be able to spend five years on the road. Having used up our vacation time, we were about to go home to Maryland disappointed at not having found the motor home for us. We had given a dealership $100 to hold one for us until the next day, but realized it just wasn't what we wanted and they gave us our money back. It was only $20,000 and the price was what grabbed us, but it just wasn't a quality product for two persons who were going to be living in it full time with all of our possessions. Then we test drove another rig twice with an individual owner. We spent a lot of time with that owner and loved the motor home, but it was obvious to us that it hadn't been well taken care of and we were afraid that if the inside was in such disrepair, that the engine had not had proper maintenance. We realized that we didn't have to buy a motor home that week because our house wasn't even on the market yet. However, just when we thought we had given up, we spotted an ad for a motor home about two hours away. We drove to Crystal River, Florida and found our motor home

 and a loving couple who became instant friends for life. It was a 35-foot, 1989 Holiday Rambler Imperial, eight years old, but it looked new to us. The couple included in their $35,000 price a 1993 Honda Civic tow car with low mileage. They had only used it when they traveled. All we had to do was go to the bank to make the transfer. The Florida couple spent two days with us, showing us everything they knew about the motor home and told us all about their travels which had to stop when the husband had a stroke. He showed us all the paperwork on the motor home, how he had taken such good care of it and explained how all the accessories worked. At that point we learned that the water tank held 30 gallons (about 250 pounds); the propane tank held 40 gallons (about 75 pounds); the gasoline tank held 50 gallons (about 400 pounds). We would have to adjust how much we carried in the motor home to take into consideration these weighty items. The wife gave us all the dishes and linens that we would need. We were excited about leaving Florida in our motor home and felt very blessed having met such a wonderful couple.

Finances

There was something we should have done differently if we had known better. We expected to sell our home quickly, so we didn't pay much attention to taking out a loan to cover the motor home purchase, believing that we would be paying it back almost immediately. We had originally planned to drive our youngest son to college in Massachusetts in the motor home and thus start our trip in August of 1997. However, we didn't get the house ready until late in July and it wasn't sold in time for us to leave in the fall. By the time the house actually settled, it had been almost a year of very high interest payments on our loan for the RV.

We did realize during the year we were getting ready to leave that it would be very beneficial for us to have as few monthly payments as possible. We would no longer have a mortgage. In our situation it was necessary for us to sell our house in order to travel. Because we had no pension monies, no retirement income, nothing coming in, we couldn't continue to pay a mortgage and travel full time, too. We found it to be unusual for couples before retirement age to be on the road full-time RVing. Nevertheless, we were very happy to have made that choice. We had originally planned to put $300,000 in the bank and live off the interest. By the time we left, we actually had less than $200,000 banked. We were able to do that much because we sold a rental property in New Jersey as well as our Maryland home. We decided that if we were doing God's work in His Kingdom that He would provide for us and He did.

During our fourth year of travel while on an expensive trip to Alaska, we were dipping into our principal. The stock market had taken a downward turn, and we were forced to consider our options. We knew we could not continue to draw from our principal so we were forced to think about ending our journey. By the time we actually stopped full-time RVing Bob had already worked part-time during visits to our hometown and while we were traveling. So after five years on the road, we decided to come back to Maryland to work.

Our biggest expenses were gasoline and insurances, especially health insurance. We could solve the gasoline problem by staying longer in one place, so instead of moving every day, we moved every week or so. Then in the winter months we stayed several months in one place. We knew when we bought the motor home that it only got five miles to the gallon, but we didn't actually understand that impact until we filled up the tank for the first time and spent $60 all at once. We had to pay health insurance as individuals. We had a plan that was not very inclusive, so fortunately we stayed healthy. To save money, we did most of our cooking in the motor home and allowed ourselves to eat out no more than twice a week. I had always done all the cooking at home, but on the road we took turns. Bob would fix all the meals and do the entire cleanup for one week; then it would be my turn. That enabled each of us to truly be on vacation every other week. It worked out nicely.

The dry runs

We knew very little about Habitat for Humanity International (HFHI) back in 1997. Bob had received some information from his college, the University of Notre

Dame about doing service work and HFHI had been mentioned. We signed up for a Habitat blitz build during June in Pikeville, Kentucky. As we had purchased the motor home by then, we decided to take it on its maiden voyage. A blitz build was one where a house was built in one week with many more volunteers than usual. Most Habitat houses were built on weekends or during weekdays with local volunteers over a period of time. In the case of the Jimmy Carter Work Project (JCWP) blitz builds, thousands of volunteers came from all over the world at the same time that President and Mrs. Carter volunteered for one week of every year. They had been helping in that way since the founders of Habitat for Humanity, Millard and Linda Fuller, drafted them eight years after the Habitat program began.

After a week of 12-hour days doing hard labor in the heat and humidity, using up our only vacation time, we built an entire house with 40 other inexperienced people, and we were hooked on Habitat. We found the other volunteers, some from the community, to be friendly and hard-working. We enjoyed meeting those we worked with, including the homeowners that HFHI referred to as the partner families, as well as those in the makeshift camping space. Our first experience with other campers was certainly a positive one. The University of Notre Dame sponsored the house we worked on by providing the money necessary, in that case, about $45,000. Many of the volunteers were also alumni of that university. The closing ceremony with Millard and Linda Fuller and President and Rosalynn Carter was extremely uplifting. They were all extraordinary speakers and doers. Even if we hadn't already been impressed with the week of building, we certainly were stimulated by that final event.

Our next little trip was to Pennsylvania for a weekend. That time we parked the motor home on the street and stayed inside my cousin's home. We found we really liked not having to pack a suitcase. Once we got on the road permanently, we rarely stayed inside someone else's home because our motor home bed was very comfortable and it did really feel like home. That was the only time that the motor home was dented because we let my cousin give the directions to park. He wasn't looking up, just looking at the curb, and we hit a tree branch up high. We learned from that to rely on ourselves entirely and we never had another dent.

Leaving our possessions

We got our house ready for sale. Little by little we got rid of possessions, taking several loads to the local auction. We decided that our collectibles were not really important. After the first couple of times we sorted things out, we realized we weren't missing any of our things and we couldn't tell that they were gone. We had accumulated so much during our marriage. If we were hesitant about parting with something we took a picture of it so it wouldn't be forgotten. That turned out to be unnecessary. There never was anything that we wished we'd kept. We invited all of our children to visit and take whatever they wanted before we started taking items to the auction. We rented a small storage unit, five feet by five feet by ten feet. I called dozens of places and found such a range of payments. There was one about 30 minutes from our house for $45 per month. If we paid up front for a year, we got one month free. So we kept two pieces of furniture that were my mother's, our 65 photograph albums, a hobby of mine, bookcases to put them in, hanging wall pictures, mostly of family, my sewing machine, a file cabinet with papers we wouldn't have to take with us, and boxes of odds and ends. To figure out how much we could take to the storage unit, we piled everything into one small bedroom and only allowed enough to fill a space equal to the five feet by five feet by ten feet unit. When it actually got time to leave and fill the motor home, we made three piles: things we definitely had to have with us, things we'd like to take, and things we would get rid of. It turned out that the things we'd like to take all fit, but if they hadn't, we would have given them to Goodwill. Bob had many tools that he wanted to take along to use for HFHI. Besides the tools, we thought we would need clothes, dishes, pots and pans, a few sheets and blankets, audio tapes, video tapings, cleaning products, writing paper, chemicals for the toilet, a camera, cards, puzzles, games, and a few books. As it turned out, although we rarely could use local libraries to check out books, most of the campgrounds had a take one - trade one policy on books, so we really didn't need our own. Before we left, we videotaped many movies from the television, in case we were in areas where we couldn't get television reception. That turned out to be very beneficial. We had decided not to get a cell phone because we didn't want any extra monthly expenses, so we invested in a used lap top computer so we could use free e-mail. We bought a small printer and had the perfect place in the motor home to keep them. There was a small table on top of a floor cabinet between the passenger seat and the swivel chair where the computer and printer fit. We put pieces of rubber shelf-liner (that all the camping stores sold) under the computer and printer and except in rare circumstances, they didn't move while we were traveling.

E-Mail for communication

E-mailing became a source of fun and irritation. When we started out few campgrounds had hookup arrangements for e-mailers. Sometimes there would be a place to plug in the computer in the office and there might be a charge of a dollar or so. Other times there was a cubicle in the clubhouse that was quite nice for sending e-mail. We would always read and write our e-mail in the motor home, so we only needed a few minutes on a phone line in order to retrieve and send the e-mail. Rarely was there a place where it was suitable to go onto the Internet, so we stuck with e-mail only. If we needed the Internet for some other reason, we used computers in local libraries wherever we were. It turned out to be too time consuming to read and write e-mail while at a library because we learned the hard way that once we brought up the e-mail on another computer, we couldn't get it on ours. Many times while we were using a computer hookup in a campground there would be people waiting in line so using the Internet for anything other than sending and retrieving e-mail was impractical. During our last year, some campgrounds were beginning to get the wireless system, which made Internet access more convenient and practicable.

Most of the time we had to leave the campground and go into a town to find somewhere to hook up our laptop. We discovered that what we needed was any place with a fax machine. Some businesses had multiple lines and we needed a dedicated line, so a fax-machine line would work just fine. Usually the person in the store didn't understand what we needed, so we would show them how we could hook up to their fax line in order to send the e-mail ourselves. Sometimes they would charge us what it would cost to send a fax, and sometimes they let us use their line free. Many times we went into a real estate broker's office and they were usually very nice about letting us hook up to their fax line. One time we sent e-mail from a mattress store. Frequently we found mailing stores from which to send. Two unusual circumstances come to mind.

Bob talked to the bell captain in a fancy hotel and he let him hook into his personal phone line while customers stood waiting to use the phone, so Bob tipped him for being so kind. Another time we went into a medical facility because we knew they would have a fax machine. The clerk wouldn't let us use it because she really didn't understand, but another employee overheard our conversation and gave us her address and directions to her home. She told us to go there and that her husband would be happy to let us use their home phone line. We did and he seemed pleasantly surprised. Of course there were towns where we couldn't find anywhere to get our e-mail, but mostly we were successful and had a chance to get to know some interesting people and processes through our efforts. Our e-mail address was: fujimo4@juno.com (Following You, Jesus, I'm Moving On). We had chosen Juno for our e-mail because it provided a completely free service. It had local phone numbers in many places in the country so we did not pay for server access or Internet connection fees just to send e-mail.

Phoning home

In order to reach our children we bought an AT&T rechargeable phone card at Sam's Club, so the cost of calling was less than 3½ cents per minute. We could add on any number of minutes to the card without going back to Sam's Club. We discovered that when a campground had a phone we could use, there were no extra charges to the phone card, but there were extra charges from a pay phone. Not many campgrounds had such a phone at that time but now and then a phone in the clubhouse facility was provided. Along with our Holiday Rambler Road Service plan was an emergency message service that enabled our children to reach us at any time by using a toll-free "800" number. Fortunately in our five years of full timing, they never had an emergency. We had chosen that particular road service because AAA, which we used previously for our cars didn't cover motor homes at the time we bought ours. When we bought a Holiday Rambler, there was information about the Holiday Rambler Club and its road service plan.

Our goals

As James Russell Lowell said, *"The wise man travels to discover himself."* We also wanted to travel in order to give back for all of the blessings we had both received during our lives. We thought we could begin to do that by working in God's Kingdom in various ways, but we were especially drawn to the organization of Habitat for Humanity, International (HFHI). We wanted to visit friends and relatives we hadn't seen in many years. Another aim was to visit all of the national parks. This would give us the opportunity to travel widely through our country. We also tried to see all of the major league ballparks because we had been baseball fans for most of our lives. It was the only sport to which we really paid much attention. Bob was interested in seeing all of the presidential libraries.

Bob had been brought up in the Catholic faith, attending Catholic schools from the first grade all the way through college. I had been brought up in the Protestant faith and had a public school education mostly. However, I had spent much time attending the Catholic Church. My father had died when I was five years old and my mom had remarried a man of the Catholic faith when I was seven. I admired and loved him very much and enjoyed going to Mass with him when I was young. Bob and I wanted to expand our knowledge of each other's faiths, so we decided to attend many services of various denominations during our travels. That turned out to be easier than we thought because many of the campgrounds in which we stayed presented their own church services, and many denominations were represented.

Travel plans

Now I'll bet you're wondering how we decided where to go. We picked a starting point where my aunt and uncle lived and drove straight from Maryland to New Mexico to arrive there on Christmas Day so that our college son could fly out to join us. Trying to give him various locations where he could meet us on his vacations so he could visit spots he'd never seen before was one criteria. Going to places where we could volunteer for HFHI gave us specific places to be at specific times. Most of our travel revolved around that. When we found ourselves near a national park, a baseball park, or a presidential library we toured those places. In most cases, we tried to take our time and not have deadlines. If we liked a place, we would stay. If we found something interesting along the way, we would stop. When we would e-mail friends about a part of the country we were in, we would learn from those who had already been there. They would tell us what special things to see and we usually paid attention, unless it was a museum stop. We also tried to stay in warm areas. Our Coast to Coast campground system led us to some spots. We looked up in our book to see where one of our campgrounds was located and headed the motor home in that direction. Near the end of our journey we chose our routes to see places that would help to accomplish our goals.

"Please Lord, help me be the kind of person my dog thinks I am."

— Author Unknown

Chapter Two

How the Dog Fits In

When we made the decision to travel full time, we had two dogs, a part golden retriever and a beagle. The golden retriever mix was 13 years old and he had died before we actually left. We took the beagle with us and on our first stop in New Mexico he also died of old age. A year passed before we got another dog. We found him at an animal shelter in Rockport, Texas and he was the perfect dog for our continuing travels. I had volunteered at the shelter several times and got to know Baggins a little. He was not too big for the motor home and he did not bark. That was important to us, living so close to other people. His original owner had named him after Bilboe Baggins in the *Hobbit* by J.R.R. Tolkein. When I finally read the book, the introduction to the *Lord of the Rings* series, I discovered that Baggins was of good character, although I didn't particularly enjoy the fantasy-type book.

Once we had Baggins, we started paying more attention to campgrounds, looking for better places for a dog to run. I was always on the lookout for a path that would lead to somewhere away from the campers so that I could unleash Baggins to let him run. I enjoyed walking daily, so I liked finding out-of-the-way paths for that purpose also. As soon as we pulled into a campground I walked around until I found some secluded area to go walking so that when morning arrived I knew just where to take Baggins. It often amazed me that upon first look there was not a suitable spot. More often than not, though, there was a place if I kept looking. Sometimes it would be around a lake, sometimes through the woods, sometimes down a road alongside a stream, sometimes over a hill onto a beach. Campers didn't seem to mind a dog running loose with me in sight, as long as we were not near their campsites.

In five years we encountered only one campground where there was a big enclosed doggie run near the campsites where dogs were allowed to be unleashed.

That was in San Diego, California. It happens that Baggins won't run away from me. He'll run off but not out of my sight, so I never had to worry about losing him or having him bother someone without my knowing what he was up to. I could walk at my pace, and he at his, as long as I was willing to find that special spot somewhere inside or near the campground boundaries. Now and then we would run into a campground that was completely fenced in. In some instances, going outside of the gate would be too heavily trafficked to walk there. We wouldn't stay long in a campground like that. Often if we went outside the gate, there would be plenty of room for a dog to run and not be in traffic.

Many times, at national parks in particular, there were strict guidelines regarding pets and walking paths. Even in those if we were spending the night, the rules could be bent a little. I noticed in one of the older full-time RVing books there was mention of it being difficult to find a campground that accommodates pets. We did not find that to be true but to the contrary. Only once, in South Dakota, did we stay at a campground that did not permit pets. That was during our first year out when we did not have a dog. Another campground nearby did accept pets and most graciously. They all expected the dog owners to pick up after their dog(s). That became an easy job as many campgrounds provided plastic bags, shovels and receptacles for that purpose. If you stuck your hand inside a plastic bag, picked up the dog's mess, then turned the bag inside out, it became a very simple task.

"One ship drives east and another west with the selfsame winds that blow.
'Tis the set of the sails and not the gales, which tell us the way to go.
Like the winds of the sea are the ways of fate, as we voyage along through life;
'Tis the set of the soul that decides our goal and not the calm or the strife."

— By Ella Wheeler Wilcox

Chapter Three

Our First Year - Let's Get Going!

Our Journey in 1998

**From Maryland to New Mexico, Nevada to Texas, Oklahoma to South Dakota,
Minnesota to Ohio, Kentucky to Texas**

After selling our house in Maryland, Bob joined me in New Mexico on February 10th. We fiddled with the motor home and taxes while we were still at my aunt and uncle's in Los Lunas, and left to begin our journey on February 13th. When we left Los Lunas, New Mexico we had no destination. For the first 18 months of our travels we just went wherever we happened to go. That was a very different and wonderful experience for us, not to be scheduled. We wanted to see Santa Fe, New Mexico, the state capital. It was the oldest state capital in the United States, founded in 1610 by the Spanish. Before that it had been an Indian settlement. The Santa Fe Trail was one of the main routes used by settlers to go west. It started in Saint Louis, Missouri and ended at the Plaza in Santa Fe, New Mexico. The oldest building in the United States was in Santa Fe, built about 1200. The buildings were made from mud because mud was the cheapest and most available material. A real adobe home had to have a new coat of mud every year. That was so much work for most families that the more modern houses were made of stucco.

In both Santa Fe and the old town of Albuquerque, the Indians had their wares, mostly silver and turquoise jewelry, set up along the sidewalks for bargaining with passersby. We also visited pueblos and saw where bread was baked in huge outdoor stoves. There were many interesting churches and missions in those areas too. I got to see where my grandfather on my father's side was buried. He had been one of the famous Teddy Roosevelt Rough Riders in the early days of New Mexico.

During the holidays we had visited the University of New Mexico in Albuquerque. There were little lights all along the tops of the houses and college buildings called farolitos or luminarias, made by putting sand in the bottom of a paper lunch bag to weight it. Then a candle was inserted into the sand and lit. They were very attractive on the ledges of the flat roofs. When we had first gotten into New Mexico on our way to my uncle's home in Los Lunas in time for Christmas dinner, we awakened on Christmas morning to snow, covering the cacti. The mountains were in the background at the Leasburg Dam State Park in Radium Springs, near Las Cruces, south in New Mexico. We had to take the southern route at that time because the unusual snowstorm had closed Route 40 through Albuquerque. That was one of the inconveniences of that trip west. The other two happened because of the terribly bumpy roads in disrepair in Arkansas. First the bicycles came loose from the bike rack at the back of the car, at 60 miles an hour. Fortunately, another driver alerted us before they fell off completely. The tires and rims were ruined. We removed them from the back of the car and put them into the motor home until we could have them fixed in Albuquerque. About nine o'clock on the night before Christmas Eve, all of our outside lights went out while we were driving. We had to stop and call our road service. It took the mechanic over an hour to find the problem. The plug of the main lighting wire harness had vibrated loose, but had not come unplugged, so it was hard to spot. We parked free that night at the all-night restaurant from where we had called the road service. It was again fortunate that the restaurant owners were so kind and accommodating.

From Albuquerque, we headed for Elephant Butte Lake, not too far south in New Mexico. It was a beautiful spot to camp, a state park, with a lake and mountains in the background. New Mexico had a fantastic system of state parks. You could purchase a yearly pass and visit them all, being allowed to stay in each one for a maximum of two weeks at one time. We enjoyed several of the New Mexico parks for a day or two and someday hoped to spend an entire summer there, from state park to state park, perhaps even returning as campground hosts. You can revisit ones you have stayed in before as long as you only remain for two weeks at one time.

We drove toward Arizona and stayed a few days at a Coast to Coast campground that was in the campground system to which we belonged. Those were the ones we tried to stay at the most because they were the least expensive, at five dollars per night. In order to belong to Coast to Coast and stay in campgrounds all over the country and Canada for five dollars per night, we paid yearly dues of $49 to Coast to Coast and we also paid yearly dues of $60 to one specific campground, called our home park. We had so much fun at those campgrounds. Different activities were planned and when we went to an ice cream social one evening, there was a live two-man band playing. Then we passed a motor home with a sign out, saying: "Relaxed Bridge?" So we set a date later to play with the couple who had the sign and they turned out to be the perfect bridge players for us. We took a day trip to Tombstone, a thriving town made to look like the Old West, with toothless cowboys standing on the corners and Big Nose Kate's Saloon where Wyatt Earp and many others used to drink. We saw the OK Corral and the Bird Cage Theater where the ladies of the night used to take their men. They had to be licensed and in a 10-year period there were over 4,000 licensed! We traveled on down into Mexico and found a lot of run-down stores and border crossings. On our way back, we stopped at a cactus farm in Bisbee, Arizona. We got back to the campground in time for a free steak dinner, the steaks cooked to order on an outside grill. Often a campground would offer a free dinner or free camping in order to influence you to buy into one of their camping packages. After dinner a couple invited us to their casita and taught us how to play hand and foot, a canasta-type card game, which was a popular game among campers, in addition to dominoes, cribbage, rummy, euchre, and pinochle. We could tell right away that we would enjoy that lifestyle. It had been two months since Bob stopped working and it looked like he would be able to get used to it!

Next we stayed with friends in a very comfortable atmosphere in Phoenix, Arizona while we waited for our mail and our settlement papers on the house. Bob had sold it on February 1, 1998. The countryside in Arizona was beautiful, mountains wherever we looked. I loved the many varieties of cacti and the neighborhoods and yards were so full of them. It was so different from back home in Maryland. We had been trying to find warm, even hot weather and had been thus far unsuccessful. Everywhere we went the cold and wind seemed to follow us.

We spent about three weeks in Nevada, did some gambling (won a few nickels) and enjoyed the cheap buffets. Casinos offered such deals. We had our six-year-old grand-daughter Ashley for a weekend and then again for an entire week and it had been just great getting to know her. We had hardly seen her up until that time. Her dad and mom lived in Henderson, near Las Vegas, about 60 miles east of Pahrump where we stayed at Preferred RV Resort. We had two 70-degree days and even went swimming, but then it turned very cold, windy, and rainy. Just like Baltimore, the temperatures changed suddenly and drastically. We had been playing lots of bridge and learning cribbage and we visited a horse ranch. Horses were not kept in barns in Nevada. Instead they stood out in the open, sometimes having a pole-barn roof over their heads. We met a lady when we played bridge at Preferred who had come to Pahrump from Hawaii at age 75 after her husband had died and decided to breed Peruvian Paso horses which she did at her Alamo Ranch. We felt fortunate to be able to see those horses being trained and could see why they were famous for their smooth gait.

We also went to Death Valley National Park that was mostly in California, slightly on the Nevada border. It is the driest and the hottest place in the Western Hemisphere, often getting above 120 degrees. It is the largest national park in the contiguous United States with over three million acres. Inside was Badwater, at 282 feet below sea level, the lowest point in the Western Hemisphere. We could see most of the park from Dante's View and noticed the desert with its unusual wildlife and scenery. We happened to be there at a spectacular time for wildflowers. The Visitors Center offered an informative presentation and displays that described the history of Death Valley, a fascinating place to visit even though it had an unpleasant name. One of our favorite places within Death Valley National Park was Scotty's Castle, the home of a famous prospector with a good story.

Death Valley's greatest legend, Walter Scott, ran away from his Kentucky home to join his brother on a ranch in Nevada. Scotty, as he was called, was hired to work as a cowboy in the Wild West show and he did that for 12 years. Then he began gold prospecting. Scotty convinced several wealthy out-of-town businessmen to give him enough money to extract ore, from a gold mine in Death Valley. Although Scotty wasn't very successful at prospecting, he lived the high life, as though he'd had great luck. He became friendly with Albert Johnson, one of his investors. Mr. Johnson came out to look at the gold mine, and didn't seem to mind that Scotty never showed it to him. The dry, sunny climate improved Mr. Johnson's health and he decided to stay. That led to his building the Death Valley Ranch, later referred to as Scotty's Castle. Scotty told everyone that it was he who was building a $2 million home. Mr. Johnson actually agreed to Scotty's boasts. The castle/hotel became a tourist fascination due to the fame of Death Valley Scotty. From the 1920s when it was built until the present, the legend of Scotty has attracted many tourists, although he died in 1954.

After Nevada, we spent time in California around the Palm Springs area and headed to San Diego from there. Everywhere we went the scenery got better and more spectacular and the people were always so friendly. We waited in the Southern California area to hear whether or not our son, John was coming to Los Angeles to visit his University of Southern California (USC) roommate in April. At Bob's birthday dinner, we got to meet William Devane, a famous actor, at Devane's Italian Restaurant in Indio, California. Often we stopped in the American Legion where Bob was a member in order to get tips about sightseeing in the local communities.

 In Joshua Tree National Park in Twenty-nine Palms, California, there are thousands of Joshua trees and huge boulders piled together in many breathtaking formations. We saw mountain climbers at a distance. When our son, Joshua was born, we planted a tree and always called it the Joshua tree, but it was actually a birch. We visited Indian Palm Canyon and took a four-mile hike through palm trees along a stream. We felt like we were in the jungle. An advertising firm was filming a car commercial with the beautiful scenery in the background. In California, wineries were everywhere we went. Driving along windy Route 78 we saw magnificent orchards and cacti, and many rows of grapes up high off the ground all along the road.

While we were staying in various campgrounds waiting for John to fly out to California, we met a couple who had been full-time RVing for 28 years. They had a small Class C motor home and while the husband drove that, the wife drove the car because their motor home was too small to tow the car. Every year they traveled from California to Maryland where they owned a small shopping center. The amazing part was running into them another time. That was the only time on our journey that anything like that happened. When we did get together with John we all attended the Jay Leno show in Burbank, California. The next day we went to a Baltimore Orioles baseball game against the Anaheim Angels at Edison International Field of Anaheim. It had an interesting entranceway supported by large bats and baseballs.

Then we headed back to Pahrump, Nevada, the state being named for its snow-covered mountains that we could view whenever we walked around the desert areas in Pahrump or traveled from Pahrump to Las Vegas. We spent three weeks with our son, Loren and Ashley, our granddaughter and her mom, Brandi, and wandered around Las Vegas some more. As our Coast to Coast package included RPI, we could stay at Preferred RV Resort in Pahrump for one week under Coast to Coast and a back-to-back second week under RPI. If we had only had one of those programs in our system, we would only have been allowed to stay one week at a time and a total of two weeks in one year at the same resort. It made it easy for us to find campgrounds in our system while we were traveling around Southern California and Nevada. We could go back and forth in the many Coast to Coast campgrounds in those areas.

We toured the Pahrump Valley Vineyards, the only winery in Nevada. It seemed a strange idea to create a winery in the Mohave Desert, but it worked and eventually had a gourmet restaurant as well as a tour of the winery and a tasting room. The tour included big vats of juice from grapes that had been processed. After the juice had been aged, the wine was bottled. You could have a bottle labeled with your own name. As we were leaving I happened to notice a name in the guest book that I recognized from college, but I didn't see anyone I knew. There was one other couple in the lobby so I asked them if they knew my friend from college. It turned out that it was my college friend, but he had lost 100 pounds and I didn't recognize him until he spoke. It was a great reunion. They had taken a year's leave from work in Chicago and bought a motor home in order to travel for a year. During our five years on the road we saw them several times, in Las Vegas, Chicago, Baltimore and Florida. The friendship among the four of us had taken an unexpected pleasant turn.

On our way out of Nevada we went by the truly extraordinary Hoover Dam, which was completed in 1935. It is located near Boulder City on the border of Nevada and Arizona, 726 feet above bedrock, the highest concrete dam in the

Western Hemisphere. The dam controls floods, stores water for irrigation and provides hydroelectric power, and is a habitat for wildlife and fish. Lake Mead, America's largest man-made reservoir, is backed up 110 miles behind Hoover Dam. Bob and I had both toured there previously on a business trip so we did not stop because we were in the motor home and it was hard to maneuver on those winding roads. It would be best to visit Hoover Dam in a car or on foot. They have a large Visitors Center and you can take a tour, which includes an elevator ride to the bottom where the turbines are located.

In the northwest corner of Arizona is the Grand Canyon National Park, a great chasm through the rocks of the Colorado Plateau. Its beauty and vast size were astounding to us. We had the extraordinary opportunity to take a helicopter ride over the canyon. On Route 40 in Eastern Arizona we drove through the Petrified Forest National Park, a fascinating land of the world's largest and most colorful concentrations of petrified wood. Petrified wood is a real wood that has taken 200 million years to form rock composed of quartz crystals that were very brittle. Within the park's 93,533 acres is the Painted Desert, at the north end of the park, full of archeological sites and 225-million-year-old fossils. The Painted Desert refers to a rainbow of colorful sandstone and mudstone layers in a narrow, crescent-shaped arc. When sediments were deposited slowly, oxides of iron and aluminum became concentrated pinks, reds, and oranges in the soil. When sediments were deposited rapidly, oxygen was removed from the soil to form grey, blue, and lavender layers.

After passing through Phoenix, Arizona and El Paso, Texas, we visited the Carlsbad Caverns in New Mexico. We had heard they were the biggest and the best and they were spectacular. The caverns contain 83 caves. It includes the nation's deepest cave and the third longest. The creation of the cavern began 250 million years ago. We spent a couple of days hiking through caves. We hiked 1-1/4 miles down into the Great Room of the Carlsbad Caverns the first day. The Great Room is 1,800 feet long and 250 feet wide. That was one of three walking tours in the caverns. At eight o'clock that evening we watched 350,000 Mexican Freetail bats come out of the cave while a park ranger talked about them. It was an awesome sight. They migrate from Mexico to give birth and then return to Mexico for the winter months. There are about 300 bats per square foot when they are sleeping inside the cave. On the second day we hiked 500 feet up for one-half mile in order to get to the mouth of the Slaughter Cave where we met guides. It was 110 degrees and a difficult hike in that heat. Of the eight who went up, the one who got sick was a slim, athletic looking young woman. Heat exhaustion is a strange phenomenon. We saw the third largest column in the world inside that cave, made when stalagmites met the stalactites. The second largest is also in New Mexico and the first largest is in China. Little did we know then that the hike up that mountain was just a prelude to 105-degree temperatures that were coming.

On a warm evening we found a little league baseball game to watch from the bleachers. We often stopped in small towns where we could do that. We didn't know the teams or fans but enjoyed the atmosphere of the game and realized that all over our great country the game was the same and the fans were the same and we enjoyed that fellowship of being together, just hanging out on a pleasant evening.

We wanted to take a tour of the Waste Isolation Pilot Plant (WIPP) in Carlsbad, but we were not allowed at the nuclear waste site because they only had tours on certain days with advance notice and we weren't there at the appropriate time. We did go into the reception area and saw a film about the underground facilities that we found very interesting. At the time of our visit, the facilities were empty due to legal problems between the states and federal government over the transportation of nuclear waste to the storage site.

We drove through the Guadalupe Mountain National Park in Salt Flat, Texas where the 8,749-feet-high Guadalupe Peak stood. We continued on our way to San Antonio, Texas where we saw briefly the Alamo and the River Walk, both great, but the heat kept us from walking around too much. Instead we opted for the pool at the campground. We traveled to Corpus Christi, Texas and north toward Houston. On the way we spent some time in Rockport, Texas where we visited a couple dozen campgrounds trying to decide whether or not we wanted to stay for a few months the following winter. It seemed like a nice area and we thought we might be ready to stay in one place, preferably a warm place. Corpus Christi, Rockport, and Houston are all on the Gulf Coast of Eastern Texas. We tested the Rockport Beach and discovered that we could walk out as far as we wanted to and the water was still not passed our knees. It was warm and lovely.

On the way to Houston we noticed that it seemed overcast which we found out was smoke from the many fields and forests in Mexico burning for the past month. We arrived in Houston, Texas on June seventh to work on a Habitat for Humanity International (HFHI) housing project. We reported to the Houston Habitat office and warehouse and were immediately put to work. That was the pre-building phase of the Jimmy Carter Work Project (JCWP). Bob worked at the three construction sites receiving materials for the 100 houses that were going to be built during the JCWP blitz week and supervising the locations of all the house parts and containers of smaller materials. Every second house had a container like the back end of a tractor-trailer nearby with many of the supplies the house leaders would need for the building. Bob drove large forklifts and trucks while he worked with other local volunteers to get the sites ready for the blitz week. One night he was on the local television news there.

I did all types of jobs including packing boxes for each house with small plumbing supplies, loading trucks with all sorts of materials, and calling my

clean-up and recycling volunteers. I was the site coordinator for the recycling program and was responsible for the cleanup of 35 houses. I also coordinated the keys for the 100 sheds and 56 site containers so that each house leader would have the correct keys, and I answered phones. One of the crew leaders (there were four per house), canceled

on the house that was going to be built by President Carter so Bob was asked to work with President Carter as a crew leader and gladly accepted. Talk about being thrilled! He wouldn't have been asked if we had not come into the pre-build process early. God put us in a good place at the right time. The recycling that I was responsible for included the Carter house so I, too, worked with the Carters and the VIP visiting dignitaries who wanted to be able to say that they had worked on the Carter house. The Carters' work at the Habitat gains a lot of publicity for HFHI attracting many news people and photographers. President and Rosalynn Carter gave up one week each year to participate in building and their prescence brought world-wide attention to HFHI.

During those pre-build weeks, Bob and I worked 12-hour days starting at seven o'clock in the morning and the temperatures were in the high 90s with 85 to 95 percent humidity. We consumed gallons of water daily and the big concern for the blitz build week was that the 6,000 volunteers would not take enough breaks or drink enough fluids. We were asked to help with that situation when the rest of the volunteers arrived. We registered the day before the build started and got our security clearances and hoped to see a lot of the people we had worked with during the JCWP in Kentucky the year before. Registration took place at the Houston Convention Center and most of the out-of-town volunteers were housed at the three large local universities including Rice University and the University of Houston. The local Houston Habitat staff had been working for a year to get everything ready. It was really amazing to see what it took to build 100 homes in one week. The transportation logistics alone were overwhelming. You can just imagine how blessed we felt to be part of such an undertaking.

We stepped into the Convention Center on Sunday afternoon where we had dinner and speeches by President Carter, Millard Fuller and Texas Governor George W. Bush. We also attended orientation meetings to meet our house leader and get our job assignments. We ran into the guys from the Notre Dame alumni house where we worked the year before. It was good to see familiar faces, especially Father Jim. We got our picture taken for our hometown newspaper. That was so there could be extra publicity all over the country. There were people from all over the world and a group sponsored an international house where they had people with many different languages working together. (We also registered and signed up for evening activities that we ended up missing by working on the house.) We were seated at dinner with the Carters and the other workers from our house. After dinner, instead of going to see a concert, President Carter asked our group to go out to the site and begin working on drilling holes in the walls so they would be ready to go up at seven o'clock the next morning when everybody was allowed to begin putting the already constructed walls up. So we all went out there even though we weren't in work clothes and some of us had sandals on. We saw the saddest looking dogs that night. I called one Houston and wanted to adopt him but after that night we never saw her again. We got home about 10 o'clock at night after dropping off people at their dorms. We stayed at a campground with about 15 other RVers, many of whom we had met in Kentucky. Bob and I just could not seem to get to sleep so we only got four hours of sleep that first night. It must have been the excitement.

We arrived on Monday morning to see slabs of concrete on the ground with a few pipes sticking up and materials all over the site. By that evening there were 35 houses framed with roofs decked. There was a lot of Habitat news on the television on the nights we could stay awake late enough to see it. No one got married that year, but the couple who got married on one of the roofs the prior year was there celebrating their first anniversary and was mentioned in the closing ceremonies. We worked on the Carter house on Monday, right alongside President and Mrs. Carter. I offered them water once and discovered the routine of having to open the cans of water for them. I wasn't around the Carter house much because my job was to oversee the trash and recycling in the whole site of 35 houses. I got that job because of being there a week early and was asked to make phone calls to set up a waste meeting with a lot of the local people. I also had worked on recycling at the Kentucky build where I had a very good teacher. I met a lot of nice people who really worked hard trying to clean up all the trash and get the cans, vinyl siding, cardboard, wood scraps and Styrofoam recycled.

Bob worked as a crew leader, getting up walls, then the trusses, then the plywood on the roof. The only problem was the oppressive heat. All week it was close to or over 100 degrees with no shade until some inside work on the house could be done. They ran out of water for us on Tuesday. There had been 100,000 aluminum cans of water donated for the entire week but it wasn't enough in that heat. It was unusual to see water in cans and I took pictures of them with the Habitat logo on them. Of course, they soon had us bottled water for the rest of the week. There were lots more problems that year with people passing out because the site was right in downtown Houston and there was just nowhere to hide from the sun. The streets were so congested with so many people working, so much material being delivered and trucks in and out to do electrical and plumbing inspection work. Volunteers were trying to get in with snacks and water for the workers. It was a real madhouse.

Every day had a specific schedule of work that had to be accomplished before we could go home in order for the house to be completely finished by Friday. On Monday we all were supposed to get the shingles on so that dry wall could be done on Tuesday. We had about 20 workers on each house when we had had about 50 the year before. Several of the 35 houses on our site did not have trusses begun by the time six o'clock came and a storm with lightning blew up. Everybody kept working anyhow. The lightning stopped and when a house was finished, their house leader would send crew members to help with someone else's house. A lot of volunteers began taking the shuttles back to dorms around four o'clock in the afternoon because the heat was so ugly. President Carter made it clear that he did not want us to leave until our shingles were on. Another lightning storm hit and the Habitat construction manager insisted that everybody get off the roofs and go home, so at about eight o'clock we did. The shingles waited until morning. That was the first rain that Houston had in 75 days. The heat was a very unusual situation for Houston in June. The high 80s and low 90s was more typical, so we broke heat and drought records while we were there. Bob and I seemed to have hit record lows and/or highs everywhere we had traveled since we left home. After making it to the showers and climbing into bed with every muscle aching, Bob with his shins cut up pretty badly, we immediately fell asleep to be back up at six o'clock in the morning and on the site by seven o'clock. Even in that terrible heat and with such long hours, it was refreshing to be around positive people who weren't complaining.

President Carter's house leader was always LeRoy Troyer, an architect from Indiana and good friend of Mr. Carter. LeRoy had a good friend also from Indiana who was a house leader for the first time, on the Notre Dame student house. That was the first time that a group of students had sponsored a house in a JCWP. Although that house

leader, Art Moser, was in the construction business, he did not know how to organize 23 inexperienced students, including 19 girls. President Carter asked Bob if he would move to the Notre Dame student house to help Art Moser. Bob was delighted because it was next to the Notre Dame alumni house where lots of people we knew from the last year's Habitat in Kentucky were working. Also it was wonderful being around those motivated, caring kids. Bob was especially good at organizing inexperienced helpers and keeping everyone busy. Except for their house leader they had no one on the house who knew anything about construction so they were very far behind on their house. The crew leaders were teachers from the college, also without building experience. Bob spent most of the week on the student house and I was back and forth among all the houses, doing recycling and trash pick up.

On Thursday night we were scheduled to see the Houston Astros play the Saint Louis Cardinals and hopefully watch Mark McGuire hit another home run at the Astrodome. We talked to someone we had met in Kentucky the year before and found out that he was a house leader that year in Houston on one of the houses called a satellite because it was not right with the group of 35 houses which included the Carter house, the Dow house, both Notre Dame houses, the Shell house, and the Continental and Southwest Airlines houses along with several local churches which had sponsored their own houses. (Each house had a sign in front of it while we were building to tell who had sponsored it.) That fellow was several blocks away and because of that, security was not as good as it could have been. When he had arrived on Monday morning some of his materials had been stolen so he got a very late start and was very behind by Thursday. Bob got someone from Notre Dame to go with us and we helped him until eight-thirty. We got to the baseball game in time for the last inning. It had been an exciting game with Mark McGuire hitting his 33rd-season home run before we arrived and it went 550 feet. We were amazed by the Astrodome. It seemed huge. The field and the stands just looked so big maybe because they were under cover or maybe because they were really huge.

Friday was quite an experience. That was the day that President Carter and Rosalynn went from house to house about three o'clock in the afternoon, blessing each house and each owner and giving them their house keys, a Bible, and saying something special to each one. Each homeowner (partner family as they were called by HFHI) had been screened prior to selection. In order to own a Habitat home, one must never have owned any home before. One must have enough of an income to pay a mortgage but not have too much income. One must work a number of sweat-equity hours, mostly of manual labor, before being allowed to move into the house. Some affiliates expected a number of sweat-equity hours to be completed even before the homeowner could apply. HFHI held the mortgage and there was no interest. The first mortgage was set for the amount of the cost of the house, property and some additional monies for the affiliate. The second mortgage was based on the difference between the first mortgage and the actual value of the house and property based on its value in that area. That prevented the new homeowner from selling within the first few years in order to make a windfall profit and taking the equity money that may have existed. The second mortgage was completely forgiven once the first mortgage had been paid off. Each affiliate had its own way of figuring out when to forgive the second mortgage. An affiliate of HFHI was an independent nonprofit organization that operated within a special service area and within the framework of the HFHI Affiliate Covenant. It was a local grass roots organization in partnership with HFHI. The local organization ran on its own although there was a manual and help if asked for, from HFHI.

The Carters had been working just like the rest of us everyday and some evenings too. We didn't know how they could stand to be in that heat on Friday afternoon walking from house to house, 100 of them on three different sites. When they got to our house, the Carter House, sponsored by Friends of Habitat, he took us all inside, away from the media, and talked to us and to the couple getting the house and to the Fullers, the couple who began HFHI 22 years before in 1976. The Carters had each of us sign a board that President Carter then hung on a prominent wall for the homeowners to remember those who had worked on their house. He had designed and dated it with a Habitat house drawn next to all the names. Tears were in the eyes of both President and Mrs. Carter as the keys were presented, a chance at a new life for the partner family, a couple and their three children. A few of the volunteers and the homeowner also sobbed. It was a very moving scene. At the same time, being cooped up in the house in that heat with 35 people was the hottest we had been all week. Being with the Carters and the Fullers had its appeal. In front of everybody, President Carter recognized Bob by name for sacrificing his time at the Carter house to help out on the other house where they needed him even more than the Carters did. That was an amazing moment for us, to be favorably singled out by a former President of the United States.

There were closing ceremonies Friday night at the biggest church we had ever seen, the First Baptist Church of Houston, built to hold about 6,000 people. We almost thought we were back in the Astrodome. We were told stories about some of the individual families and the circumstances that qualified them for a first home of their own. We listened to Millard Fuller and Jimmy Carter speak and they were both so moving. It was the high point of the week, as it was in the past year also when we participated in the Kentucky JCWP. Working our unused aching muscles and working in such heat became very worthwhile as we sat there and heard about those deserving homeowners and about all of us working together to make things better for someone else.

Some companies not only sponsored (provided the money) but also sent people from their company to be the volunteers on the sponsored house. Others, volunteers using their vacation time, paying their own transportation, contributing $250 to Habitat for the privilege of volunteering with President and Rosalynn Carter and other famous people who came to help, working their hearts out, told us that they never felt better about giving all that away. It was the way we felt also. It was an indescribable and truly wonderful feeling! We talked to a lot of people who didn't feel they could afford it, but went away saying that they were thinking about how to work it out for the next time. Often God would work it out for us if we would only ask. There was one man present who had never missed a JCWP.

We really enjoyed the city of Houston. In addition to getting to see the Astrodome, we were taken to Transco Park where there was a strange looking man-made wall of water falling. There was no visible source of water coming to it. The sight was a spectacular one. We got an opportunity one night to eat dinner at Rice University. From the seventh floor of the dormitory we could see the entire campus. It was quite a view, a college right in the midst of a big city, much like the University of Southern

California in the midst of Los Angeles, where our son, John graduated. John had actually applied to Rice University but we had never been on the campus before.

We took a couple of days to recuperate from cuts, bruises, sore muscles, aches, and sunburn. Then at the end of the week and into the next few weeks, Bob and I helped out with punch lists. Those were items put on a list that needed to be completed in each house. Some of the house leaders had taken Friday flights out of Houston before their houses were completely finished. There were lots of odds and ends to accomplish throughout the three build sites. I particularly liked doing that sort of work because there was no time limit. During the time we worked on punch lists, we hooked our motor home up to the electricity at the Houston Habitat office. Few of the volunteers who came in for the JCWP blitz week 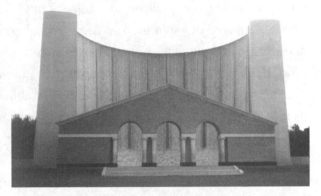 could stay, so we were glad to help out a few of the locals to make it possible for 100 families to move into their new homes on June 27, 1998. It was just awesome, realizing that we were part of helping them, including 260 children to reach the goal of home ownership for the first time. The families had been screened and chosen months before through a long, thorough process. They would continue to have advisors look in on them for a couple of years to come. The families we met appeared to be very grateful. They would have mortgages that they could afford, held by Habitat. As they paid back the money, Habitat would use it to build more homes. Some of the families would pay interest-free mortgages that were less than their previous rent. That gave them the opportunity to build better lives for their children.

Between working on punch lists and leaving Houston, we did some sightseeing there. As guests of the Habitat office, the construction manager and his wife took us to the Houston Space Center and Moody Gardens, which included a 10-story Rainforest Pyramid displaying an amazing tropical environment. That is where birds and tropical fish share the lush environment with exotic plants from the rainforests of Africa, Asia and the Americas. It is on the outskirts of Galveston. We toured around the Galveston area at the beach also.

When we began our travels again, near Huntsville, Texas on Route 45 we passed an enormous statue of Sam Houston, as tall as the tallest trees in that area. We saw many small grass fires along the roads and passed the beautiful Dallas Skyline. We found the neatest place in Davis, Oklahoma. It was called Turner Falls Park and it was located on a river with a huge swimming hole in the middle. You could walk on the rocks throughout the river, go diving or wading, camp, all in a beautiful setting. It was the first time we enjoyed being in the 100-degree weather. We found a shady spot and a breeze and went in and out of the water. There were no rules, it seemed. People had rafts, tubes, food, dogs, and we saw no signs saying "no jumping, no this or that". It was the first time I had done any diving from a high dive in about 11 years. It took some courage, but as a youngster I had learned to dive before I learned to swim. Our next Oklahoma stop was to dry camp on a fishing lake with nice scenery. In another Oklahoma campground we learned about a group of campers called *Loners On Wheels*. They were older singles who got together frequently in order to share food and fun. One of the ladies had a dummy sitting in the passenger's seat so it would appear that she had a traveling companion. We discovered while in Oklahoma that the Baltimore Orioles were playing the Texas Rangers at The Ballpark in Arlington. It took us nearly three hours to drive there from the campground but we went two nights in a row. We went early the first night to see the warm-ups and met an usher from Delaware. Although we had bought the cheapest tickets, he let us stay in the better seats and told us if we came back the next night, he'd seat us again. We enjoyed watching our Orioles play someplace besides at home.

At that point we bought a book at Camping World, the store chain across the country that most campers use, to give us suggestions about free campsites. After trying out a few and either not being able to find them or having had them change from overnight camping to day permits only, or being so remote, we decided we had spent more on gasoline than it would have cost to pay for a closer campground, so we stopped looking for free campsites.

Next we headed west to Dodge City, Kansas to learn all about the Old Wild West. One fact interesting to us was that the old television show *Gunsmoke* was not filmed in

Dodge City. It was there, however, that we had trouble picking up our mail. We had a mail service based out of Cincinnati, Ohio with a camping organization called Family Motor Coach Association (FMCA) that sent our mail to wherever we told them we were staying. That was a free service so we only had to pay for the postage. We called an 800 number to notify them where to send our mail. One could only belong to FMCA if he/she had a motor home. At that time they didn't allow fifth wheel or trailer owners to become members. If we weren't staying long enough in one campground or were staying in a campground that didn't accept guest mail, we gave the mail service the name of a post office in a town where we knew we would be going at a future date. The post office would hold our mail for 30 days as general delivery. This was only the one time when it didn't work out as planned. Our mail didn't reach the post office before we arrived and still wasn't there when we left, so we asked the post office to forward it to the next town we planned to be in. That was the only glitch we had with mail service in our five years on the road. In our case, none of our children volunteered to send us our mail and using that service worked well for us.

The 100-degree temperatures followed us for six weeks until we reached Kansas City, Missouri where the quick change in temperature into the low 70s was a relief. We stopped at a campground there that had the most unusual pool/lake situation we could have imagined. The pool was huge, with a long lap area, a diving area, and twice the size of those two put together, a shallow area. The shallow area went right to the beach. There was chlorinated water over sand in one part. We couldn't figure out how they kept the sand from going into the pool part, but except for a couple of inches, it didn't seem to. It rained while we were there, so we didn't get to try it out. It dried up enough one evening so that we could go to the Kansas City Royals Kauffman Stadium which had been renamed in 1993 from Royals Stadium. In 1973, when Kauffman Stadium opened, it was way ahead of its time. The most outstanding feature that we noticed was the 12-story scoreboard, in the shape of the Royals' crest, located beyond the center field fence. In left-center field, there was a huge JumboTron video board. Natural grass gave the field an intimate feel. The seats were blue and all faced second base. We had a great view of the enormous fountains and the Midwest landscape beyond the outfield fence.

As we drove through Kansas and Missouri to Nebraska, we were surprised not to have found corn for sale everywhere. We finally found a produce stand selling corn on the cob but thought it was weird in corn country not to have found it more readily, as we always had corn in Maryland by July Fourth and that was mid-July. We learned later that most of the corn grown was for animal feed. Boys Town USA, originally known as Father Flanagan's Boys' Home was in Omaha, Nebraska. We toured the grounds and were very impressed with the students we met and the wide range of behavioral health services that were offered.

We had perfect weather in the mid-80s and sunny when we tried to pick up Joshua, our youngest at the Sioux Falls, South Dakota airport. He wasn't on the expected flight so after a four-hour wait he came in on a re-routed flight. There had been a storm and flooding in the Minneapolis area that slowed down many of the air flights on August ninth. He had transferred in Minneapolis from Boston. When he got off the plane, Joshua had Chesapeake Bay blue crabs packed in dry ice as a surprise for us. He knew how long it had been since we had eaten hard crabs. That was a great treat and the three of us enjoyed every morsel. We traveled with Joshua across the state of South Dakota and saw acres and acres of sunflowers. The yellow fields were gorgeous. We passed hundreds of motorcyclists traveling from the yearly South Dakota Biker Rally in Sturgis, South Dakota. That was surely a sight to see! We camped in the Badlands National Park where the rock formations were unusual and some reminded us of the Grand Canyon. We took the car into a seven-mile stretch that few cars were

traveling. We really needed a four-wheel-drive vehicle, but our little Honda Civic worked out okay. It was a dirt road and the width of a one-lane sized narrow road forcing us to go almost into a ditch to give way to an oncoming car. It was worth it for the views. That night we met two girls, each traveling alone in a car with a little pup tent, so we all got together and played Balderdash and had lots of fun getting to know them. We took a day to see Mount Rushmore National Park in Rapid City, South Dakota where we were enthralled with the presidents: George Washington, Thomas Jefferson, Theodore Roosevelt, and Abraham Lincoln. It was extremely interesting to learn about the history that went into making that memorial designed by Gutzon Borglum. We saw it by day and by night with a lighting ceremony. We were told that Mount Rushmore is the greatest free attraction in the United States.

We also viewed the Crazy Horse Memorial to North American Indians. It is a project in progress, which was started in 1948 by a private foundation. After learning what was involved to even begin the sculpting on the mountain, we understood why it was taking so long. There are no federal or state monies being used, so progress is sometimes delayed because of the lack of funds. The man who began Crazy Horse, Korczak Ziolkowski, died in 1982 and his wife and 10 children are some of the relatives working on it. They hope to reach completion in a couple more decades. They spend much of their time trying to raise funds to continue the work. It is a much larger undertaking than the presidents. All of the mountain sculptures were incredible to us.

To encourage citizens to see the national parks, the government issues passes that admit the pass holders and any accompanying passengers in a private vehicle free. The pass is good for a 12-month period and can be purchased for $50 at any national

park where an entrance fee is charged. Some were free and the most costly charged $20. Most are somewhere in between, many at five dollars. There is also a senior citizen pass that is good for life but we didn't qualify for that at the time.

We drove through Custer State Park, full of large straight-up rocks, curves and tunnels.

We saw buffaloes, deer and mules where there was open land. We stopped to take close-up photographs of long-horned sheep. Wind Cave National Park, just outside of Custer in Hot Springs, South Dakota has one of the world's largest and most complex caves, well known for its outstanding display of boxwork, an unusual cave formation composed of thin calcite fins that resembled honeycombs. The park also has nearly 30,000 acres of mixed-grass prairie, almost gone in our country. There was so much to see in that part of South Dakota that the week just flew by before Joshua had to return to the Sioux Falls Airport. Bob and Joshua did have a chance to play golf at an Air Force Base near Rapid City, South Dakota. After seeing Joshua off, we spent a couple of days at a nearby truck stop while the motor home was being serviced. We met many truckers in the lounge provided by the truck stop. It was interesting to watch the Clinton impeachment hearings with many opinionated truckers.

Driving through Minnesota we picked up our mail and had a letter from a friend from Pahrump, Nevada who was coming to visit her daughter in Wisconsin. As that was the direction in which we were headed, they came to visit us at our campground. When we realized we were so close to the Chicago area, we took a couple of days to drive down there to visit Bob's sister and my college friend and his wife. We had the opportunity to watch the Baltimore Orioles play against the Chicago White Sox at Comiskey Park II. This is where we saw the ballpark that was built right next to the old Comiskey Park and named the same, after the White Sox original owner, Charles Comiskey. We particularly liked that all the seats were blue, with four levels of seats extending from in back of homeplate to the foul poles. The upper decks seemed very steep. A replica of the old park's famous scoreboard showed fireworks and bombs exploding.

Next we took a four-hour-ferry ride from Manitowoc, Wisconsin to Ludington, Michigan instead of taking the motor home all the way around Michigan. It seemed eerie to be out in the middle of Lake Michigan without being able to see land or other boats anywhere for about three of the four hours across the water. Once off the ferry, we headed to Grayling, Michigan to stay with a friend who had moved there from Maryland. In the northern part of the state, Grayling has the Au Sable River winding through the town. We toured a logging camp museum at the Hartwick Pines State Park, the largest state park in the Lower Peninsula of Michigan. The museum shows the past importance of Michigan's pine lumber industry. It is an unusual outside museum, along a trail.

In Clinton, Michigan we spent time with college friends near Dearborn where Ford Motor Company operated. Our friends own an 80-acre tree farm with lots of privacy. We visited the Ford Museum on 93 acres, built to credit Americans with enterprise and innovation by documenting three centuries of technological and cultural change. There was a private collection of motorcars, airplanes of the Wright Brothers, many modes of transportation, furniture from early presidents, a display of violins, exhibits of communication, industry, agriculture and domestic life as well as a commemoration of Thomas Edison for his career of inventions. We could watch demonstrations including those of blacksmithing, glassblowing, and pottery making. There were rides on a steam train, horse drawn carriages, sleighs, a carousel, and a paddlewheel steamboat. In the evening we attended a baseball game in Detroit at Tiger Stadium. We were there a few years after the major renovations in 1993 when a food court was included. There were still columns in front of some of the blue and orange seats. The overhang in right field provided homeruns that would not be homeruns in other stadiums. Tiger Stadium seemed like a ballpark from the early 1900s with natural grass growing. We liked the way the Tiger mascot was painted on the walls next to the ramps going to the seats. We also went to Tony Paco's in Toledo, Ohio, just across the border. If you were a M*A*S*H fan, you might remember that Klinger was from Toledo and often mentioned Tony Paco's hot dogs.

There was a 32-room bookstore in Columbus, Ohio where friends from our old Catonsville, Maryland neighborhood took us when we visited them. Then we stayed with friends near Dayton, Ohio. When we stayed with friends like that, we parked our motor home on their property and spent the night in it hooked up to their electricity. During the day we spent our time with them inside their homes and did our sightseeing with them. We preferred to sleep in our motor home.

In November we went down to Mammoth Cave National Park in Kentucky, which was established to preserve the largest recorded cave system in the world with more than 360 miles explored and mapped. It took us two hours to go two miles and 400 steps to see the cave. That was one of the most beautiful areas of Kentucky.

Our Coast to Coast home park was called Breckinridge Lake Resort. Members could stay at their own home park for two weeks completely free. So we took advantage of that and stayed there in Crossville, Tennessee. Although it was a small park with no clubhouse or activities, it gave us an opportunity to catch up on paperwork and do some minor repairs on the motor home, car and bicycles, which traveled with us on a bicycle rack attached to the back of the motor home. We found some bridge players at the local senior center in Crossville and also visited a local state park, called Fall Creek Falls. It has the highest falls east of the Rocky Mountains and it was a nice hike up to see it. It was one of the prettiest sights we had seen. It was amazing when we had extra time to look around in any one area what we could find that we didn't even know existed. Breckinridge Lake was huge and beautiful. We toured the Corvette Museum in Bowling Green, Kentucky. In Gatlinburg, Tennessee, we took a day trip to the Great Smokey Mountain National Park and attended the Dixie Stampede in Pigeon Forge.

In Nashville, Tennessee we had a friend who we had met at the Houston Habitat who wanted help with a Thanksgiving dinner at a women's shelter that served 160 people. That turned out to be quite a blessing to us. It was there that we met Don Goodner who wrote the song *Angels Among Us* for the group Alabama. We never knew how God was going to bless us as we traveled.

We could not leave Tennessee without going to Elvis' home at Graceland in Memphis. It was always a special experience to be in those surroundings. Even if you are not an Elvis fan, seeing Graceland is an experience no one should miss. That time many awards had been added to the racquetball-court room, some of Elvis' cars had been removed, and there were no longer tour guides giving out information and answering questions. They had been replaced with audio-cassette guides. An additional bedroom downstairs and the kitchen had been opened to the public, but still no one was allowed upstairs. Also in Memphis was the Civil Rights Museum at the Lorraine Motel where Martin Luther King, Jr. had been assassinated in April, 1968. When we adopted our son, Rob he had no middle name and was born in 1968 of mixed-raced parents, so we gave him the middle name Martin. Memphis had its Beale Street, similar to Bourbon Street in New Orleans, Louisiana. We listened to some fun music outside while people danced in the streets.

Shortly after we got to Rockport, Texas where we had decided to winter at Lagoons RV Resort, our daughter, Robin and her fiancé, Eric came to visit us. The resort was near the Gulf of Mexico and Eric really enjoyed fishing from the docks in town. There was lots of fishing in the Rockport area and in the Aransas Bay. We had an early Christmas-present opening with them. In order to decorate the motor home for Christmas we put the wrapped packages on the dashboard before it was time to mail them to the other children. Our youngest son, Joshua came to visit for Christmas and it was good to spend time with him there. We went to the American Legion for a big Christmas dinner. We took him to see the USS Lexington in Corpus Christi, about 40 miles south of Rockport. The U.S.S. Lexington, the fifth warship to use the name Lexington, was used during World War II and again in 1955. For almost 30 years, the Lexington operated in the Gulf of Mexico as a training facility for student Naval Aviators. When she was decommissioned in 1991, the Lexington was transferred to a private organization in Corpus Christi and became a museum ship where anyone can tour the entire huge warship, as we did. Groups can also organize parties and overnights there. Its size astounded us.

We had chosen Lagoons RV Resort when we had passed through Rockport, before we went to the Houston Habitat the June before. It was being built with all the sites and streets in concrete when we signed up for three winter months. We found out that by staying in a campground for several months, even a modern one like Lagoons, we could stay as cheaply as we could stay in our Coast to Coast system. The monthly rates came way down compared to what that same campground would cost if we paid per day. When we arrived, the clubhouse and pool weren't finished and some of the sites hadn't been built yet, but our site's concrete had been poured to the specifications of our motor home as promised. We liked our site because it was on the last row next to woods and a pond. It was a good place for walking within the park, and in the city park across the road with a half-mile track. Rockport is such a flat town that we could ride our bikes everywhere. As soon as we realized that there was no recycling system at the campground we decided to begin one. With bridge every day in Rockport we kept very busy. The town had a Women's Club, a community center, a senior center, and various campgrounds, all offering bridge and other activities. Besides all that, the weather was beautiful, a great way to end the year.

"People will walk in and out of your life, but only true friends will leave footprints on your heart."

— From *A Thousand Paths To A Peaceful Life*
by David Baird

Chapter Four

Our Second Year - Exploring the USA and Canada

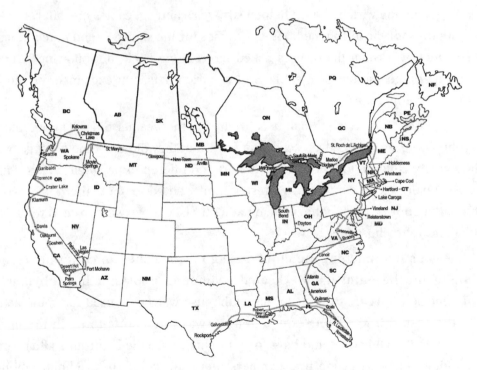

Our Journey in 1999

From Texas to Florida, Georgia to Maryland, Connecticut through Canada, Washington to Nevada

We began the year in Rockport, Texas at Lagoons RV Resort. The clubhouse was still in the process of being built and Bob enjoyed helping out. Brian and Linda Pahl had come from Kelowna, British Columbia in Canada with their three children, Jason, Derek, and Megan to build the RV resort. I organized the recycling for the campground and did some volunteer work at the Humane Society where I got Baggins on January 22, 1999. He was a four-year-old Griffon Nivernais, descended in the 1200s from the now-extinct Chien Gris de Saint Louis from France, a grey wired-hair dog with a bushy, slightly unkempt appearance, looking much like the Benji dog in the movies, having a great disposition and quiet manner.

Bob worked in the clubhouse on building the inside walls with two by fours, threading in all the wiring. I even helped strip wire and cut cables one afternoon. Bob also built tops for the telephone booths, benches for the showers, and much more. We did so much work that the owners asked us to come back the following year to be workcampers, getting our site, cable, and electric for free in exchange for our work around the campground.

Our son, John came to visit in February but the weather did not cooperate. Bob and John could not take a deep sea fishing trip, but they did do some golfing. We had invited all six children to visit us in Rockport and offered to pay their airfare that one time. We were excited about our lifestyle and wanted to show them how we were living in Rockport, a place none of them had ever visited. We were excited when Robin, Joshua and John chose to stay with us.

It was fun watching the clubhouse go from a shell of concrete to rooms, including the beautiful indoor heated swimming pool and hot tub that were finally finished in February. Part of the clubhouse was being used for some activities while the rest of it was being completed. It was interesting to be in the midst of an activity in the clubhouse and have to run home to use the bathroom. Being part of the building and part of the first campers there formed a special bond among the campers.

Many people kept dogs and cats in their motor homes and trailers but we seldom heard any noise from them. Baggins remained very quiet. Our site at Lagoons turned out to be perfect for walking Baggins behind the fence in a wooded area with a pond. We also took Baggins to the Rockport Beach on Aransas Bay for walks and swims. I had believed that all dogs liked to swim. Baggins did enjoy wading, but I wanted him to come out into the deeper water to swim with me. I had to put him on his leash and practically drag him out. I did discover that he could swim, but as soon as I took his leash off, he swam right back to shore. After awhile when he saw that I was still in the deeper water, he swam back out to me, but only long enough to check on me, then headed back to shore in a hurry. With the flat topography in the Rockport area we walked frequently with and without Baggins. We could bike just about anywhere we wanted to go.

When we left Rockport, another couple left with us in their trailer and we toured Galveston Island and walked along the sea wall together. From Rockport, Galveston Island is north on the eastern coast of Texas, southeast of Houston. It sits between Galveston Bay and the Gulf of Mexico. We dined in seaside restaurants on Galveston Bay. We walked on the concrete sea wall by the Gulf of Mexico. Perpendicular to the sea wall were piers with shops and more restaurants. In 1984 a revitalization project of Galveston Island committed 200 businesses to the downtown area. Galveston's climate during the winter months ranges from infrequent 50s to the low 80s. Besides beautiful beaches and delicious dining, Galveston also has 1,500 restored historic homes. It's a gorgeous, historic, fun place to visit.

When the four of us arrived in New Orleans, Louisiana we walked around the Market Place, had coffee au lait and beignettes, French pastries, at DuMonde's, and took a horse and buggy ride around Jackson Square in the French Quarter, the home for artists, shops and the Saint Louis Cathedral. We had a Cajun dinner at Jimmy Buffet's Margaritaville, and went to the River Walk Mall and had hurricane drinks at Pat O'Brien's on Bourbon Street.

We left our friends to go on to Montgomery, Alabama on our way to Panama City Beach, Florida. Still in Alabama, just before we got to Pensacola, Florida we watched a pick up truck blow a tire on the other side of the highway, going in the direction opposite from us. He rolled over at least 20 times - all the way across all the lanes and landed upside down on the shoulder on our side of the road. Then we watched in amazement as the young driver dragged himself out from under the truck.

We spent several weeks visiting various friends in areas of Florida. We attended Orioles spring training games in Jupiter and Fort Lauderdale and had an afternoon on Juno Beach, just beautiful at 72 degrees. The water was gorgeous. There was a huge flea market in Kissemmee, Florida, not far from Disney World in Orlando. We drove through Everglades National Park in Homestead, Florida, and saw herons, egrets, and ibis, white and graceful. The park is known for its rich bird life. Spanning the southern tip of the Florida peninsula and most of Florida Bay, Everglades National Park is the only subtropical preserve in the United States.

We had a few lovely days in Southern Georgia. I spent time just sitting outside relaxing, reading and petting the dog. Country Lakes Campground in Quitman, Georgia, was a great spot for letting Baggins run loose. We had not had a chance before to find out if he would stay with us if he were off the leash. He ran around, but he never took his eyes off of us. We took advantage of that peaceful time before going to work at Habitat in Americus, nearby.

Because Americus, Georgia is the headquarters for HFHI, they provide a free, small, five-site RV park within walking distance of the headquarter buildings for the exclusive use of Habitat volunteers. In a house at the campground built similarly to a Habitat house without the bedrooms, we did our wash free. There are phone and e-mail connections provided. It has a complete kitchen and living area. Two bathrooms both have tubs. It is very unusual to find a campground with a bathtub. Only one other time in five years did we see that. There were other people who came to Americus during the winter months to get away from the cold who were not in RVs. For volunteering their time, they received a place to live and a stipend to live on. They only had to get their transportation there. It was a good deal. Some of the winter work was in the office. Some worked in the day care center provided by HFHI for their employees and residents of the town. Often a person in transition of some sort would stay at one of the Habitat apartments in exchange for working for HFHI in one capacity or another. It provided a peaceful place to sort out one's problems and be around upbeat people. One of the jobs needed doing at HFHI surprised me. Every day someone had to open thousands of envelopes full of donations. It was amazing to us how many donations poured in every day.

By Friday of the build week in Americus, in Sumter County 25 houses were finished. Bob had been asked to be a house leader in charge of a crew of 35 volunteers and he did a good job, although he had never done that job before. He had started out working on a house made of concrete as one of the crew members, but because of a shortage of house leaders at that build, he was switched to a frame house. I spent my time doing the recycling and trash aspect of the blitz build. I worked with another older lady and a few high school students and got many bruises and very muddy. That Georgia red clay was something else. It stained everything it touched. On Wednesday of the build week, in the backyard of the house Bob and his crew were building, they surprised him with a birthday cake after lunch. It always felt like we were working alongside family members.

After the blitz build, we stayed on to help get a youth center in Plains, Georgia under roof. President Carter had asked a few of the house leaders to stay an extra week to do that in the town of 700 where he lived, about 10 miles from Americus. Bob worked hand in hand with Mr. Carter. That project was going to be called the Carter Youth Center because President and Mrs. Carter  were sponsoring it. The volunteers were provided with rooms and meals at the local Ramada Inn. One night President Carter asked Bob and me to sit down and eat with him and it was quite an experience to get to listen to him talk about his routines in Plains. He often ran his peace center in Atlanta from Plains. We attended President Carter's Sunday School Class on Easter Sunday and found him to be a very good, humorous teacher. The church was filled to capacity for his class, many more attending than at the church service afterwards. We had a surprise visit from a couple we had met at a bridge game in Kansas City, Missouri. They were on their way to Florida and decided to stop to see us, so they were with us for the Easter services and were thrilled to meet President Carter. We also had a surprise visit from Tennessee friends we had met at Lagoons. They made dinner for us in the little building on top of the hill at the little Habitat campground. If it hadn't been for e-mail, we would have missed these visits. We tried to keep in touch with many campers, volunteers, and bridge players as well as our family and friends from home.

We had gotten to know our neighbors in the five-site RV park so it was kind of hard to leave Americus after three weeks, but we were also eager to be heading home. We had taken time out to visit the POW camp in Andersonville, which was very moving. Originally it was officially known as Camp Sumter, one of the largest Confederate military prisons established during the Civil War. Today Andersonville National Historic Site is the only park in the National Park system, which memorializes all American prisoners of war throughout our country's history and commemorates the sacrifice of Americans who lost their lives in such prison camps.

We had also taken a tour of HFHI, an interesting addition to our first-hand knowledge. We went to Atlanta, visited some friends and toured the Carter Center to learn more about what the Carters do. It was a beautiful complex and included the Jimmy Carter Library. Often a presidential library takes on the personality of the individual president. The libraries have provided structure for the recent presidents for cataloging their papers. After President Coolidge, there was not enough room at the Library of Congress for the many papers of all the presidents, so the idea of each president having his own library was developed. The Carter Center, in partnership with Emory University, works on advancing human rights and alleviating unnecessary human suffering in more than 65 countries. Founded in 1982 by Jimmy and Rosalynn Carter, the staff is committed to peace, fighting disease, strengthening democracies, helping farmers, building hope, and is a nonprofit, nongovernmental organization, supported by donations. They often work with poor and forgotten people. We also went to see the Atlanta Braves Turner Field but we weren't allowed inside for a tour so we parked and peeked in through the gates.

We stayed in a truck stop before going on through South Carolina and North Carolina. Truck stops were free and often available in places where our Coast to Coast system wasn't. The problem with staying in a truck stop was that sometimes our carbon-monoxide detector would go off in the middle of the night because of the trucks' exhausts. One time we just had to leave to find somewhere else to park to get the alarm to stop. After a stay in Manassas, Virginia we drove into Reisterstown,

Maryland on April 20, 1999, the first time in our home state since we left with the motor home in December of 1997.

We had originally planned on going back for our daughter, Robin and Eric's wedding in May and decided to stay for the entire summer. It gave our youngest son, Joshua the opportunity to return to his old high school job. Our tenants had vacated the condominium we kept after my mom died so we had a place for the three of us to stay for the summer. Joshua's job was across the street so we didn't need a second car. Robin looked lovely on her wedding day with weather in the mid-70s. It took place at a bed and breakfast on a huge piece of property, beautifully landscaped, a wonderful scene for pictures. All of the boys were there except for Arn. Our granddaughter, Ashley was the flower girl. Bob and I drove with Robin's granddad in his light blue 1967 Cadillac that had belonged to Bob's dad before he died. Bob was going to surprise his sister, Karen with it when she came to stay with us for the wedding, but her cancer treatments prevented her from coming.

We attended an Emergency Medical Services (EMS) Memorial ceremony for the men and women who were killed in 1998 doing their jobs. That was the seventh year for the event, held in Roanoke, Virginia honoring EMS people from eleven different states. It was a very moving service with reminders that life certainly can be fragile and that we all have so many people protecting us that we often take for granted. The service with color guard, piano music, singing, and Taps was exquisitely done. The speaker said, "They had a flavor of life that those they protect never taste." Their motto was: "We do, that others may live". That year 27 men and women were honored. It felt so right to be there during the Memorial Day weekend holiday. We had friends there from Lagoons who had a daughter being honored and it was good to see them again.

They had told us about the service and we surprised them by remembering the date and being close enough to get there at that time. After the service we all went outside for a fly-by with two helicopters. Our friends' daughter along with two men had crashed and burned in a helicopter on their way to helping someone else. So the helicopter fly-by was appropriate. There was an impressive reception at the Roanoke Hotel. We stayed at a campground in Greenville, Virginia about 75 miles from Roanoke, where we enjoyed temperatures in the high 80s. We relaxed for a day before driving home on the Skyline Drive through the Shenandoah National Park.

From Reisterstown we drove the car to a Notre Dame Habitat blitz build in June. We were only building one house so we got to know everybody better than when I had been responsible for recycling and trash for 35 houses. The director of the Habitat affiliate in Saint Joseph County, Indiana had a terrible accident at the site. He was hospitalized on Wednesday in the middle of the build so I was given responsibility for dispensing water, setting up for snacks and lunches as well as trash and recycling. Bob had been asked to be the house leader because of his experience at the Americus build. Being the wife of the house leader made things extra special. Everybody on the build treated us with such fondness. On Thursday night of the build week, there was a Habitation ceremony. It was even more fantastic than the ceremonies we had experienced with Jimmy Carter and Millard Fuller speaking. I hadn't thought that was possible. There were four houses being dedicated at the same time. Our partner family had put the whole program together in grand style. We saw a presentation by a signing choir that was stupendous, something we had never experienced before. There was also a presentation by a drill team with ever-so-talented children of all ages. They had a drill leader calling out cadence and they intertwined Bible verses as they sang beautifully. There was also other singing by individuals with unbelievable voices, including a staff member from the local Habitat office. It was hard to take in all that talent at one ceremony. That was a time when homeowners got to thank sponsors, volunteers, and the affiliate, a time when sponsors gave thanks for the opportunity to be a part of such a wonderful cause, a time for volunteers to thank God and give praise for the part we had in it, a time of reflection, spirituality, and tears. My wish was that everyone would have an opportunity to participate in a blitz build week to be able to experience such fulfillment. The house was completed on Friday and the homeowners, the partner family, seemed overwhelmed by the process. It just amazed them that strangers would build them a house.

Aside from building during the day, we were able to play bridge every night after dinner. One of the fellows we played with who happened to bring cards was Father John, a priest recruiter. It was quite interesting to meet and get to know him. The South Dining Hall at the University of Notre Dame where we enjoyed all of our breakfasts and dinners was an event likened to nothing any of us had experienced in our college days. Most of the volunteers had previously attended the University of Notre Dame and so much had changed on the campus since they were there, particularly the addition of women on campus. There were 28 stations under one roof in the dining hall with many varieties of pasta, pizza, make-your-own stir-fry, salads, fruit, bread, rolls, make-your-own deli sandwiches, hamburgers, garden burgers, fries, roast beef, vegetables galore, baked fish, mashed potatoes, gravies, make-your-own waffles, bagels, cereals, all kinds of juices and drinks, lots of healthy choices and incredible desserts and make-your-own sundaes. We could even take ice-cream cones outside as we left. When our friends came down from Michigan for the weekend after the build week we took them to South Dining Hall and they enjoyed it so much that we went back for all the rest of our weekend meals. As they toured the campus with us, Bob realized how much it had changed since his graduation in 1967. We met several couples that were at Notre Dame with Elder Hostels, a group of senior citizens who signed up for educational courses on various college campuses across the United States. We liked that idea. They stayed in the dorms for two weeks, took classes and did some sightseeing, an inexpensive way to see our beautiful country and to keep their brains working.

On our way back to Maryland we stopped to see friends near Dayton, Ohio. Their house had always been a halfway point when we drove back and forth to Bradley University in Peoria, Illinois where I attended college. Those friends had lived in our Catonsville, Maryland neighborhood growing up. Soon after we returned from Indiana we received a note from a Pennsylvania friend we had met on the Georgia build. He had raised $1000 and paid his own way to participate in a

Habitat Global Village build in Alaska. He was very excited about the trip. Volunteers from the Global Village part of Habitat were sent to many states and to countries throughout the entire world.

The month of July flew by. We spent a week at a campground on the Jersey Shore, spending time with friends from my old hometown of Vineland, New Jersey, had time on the beach with son, John and had dinner with son, Rob. We had perfect beach weather and enjoyed the relaxation. During our beach trip in New Jersey we learned that my cousin's husband had died at age 56 after eight years of chemotherapy. We came back for the funeral that was the most moving we had ever attended. He had belonged to a support group with the Course in Miracles and several of the women in his group spoke and/or read poems about him. He had been the only man in the group and they really had valued his friendship. He was also a known Baltimore artist and had been an art teacher before he decided to become a professional artist.

We went to a 50th *This Is Your Life* celebration for Michael Hoover in Virginia. Michael was the friend we met 12 years before who worked for a living as an Elvis tribute artist. If you closed your eyes you thought you were listening to Elvis. His appearance was also similar to Elvis in the later years. We had followed him around Baltimore and Washington, DC and had him perform for Bob's 30th high school reunion in 1992. The 50th party was a surprise put on by his wife and manager and once again we were very moved by all the wonderful things various people said about his friendship as well as his talents. He sang songs for us that were not Elvis' that we had never heard before and we enjoyed his wonderful voice with such tremendous range. We kept being reminded that relationships are more precious than possessions.

We loaded up the motor home at the end of the summer to take Joshua back to Gordon College in Massachusetts. We spent a couple of nights in the parking lot at the college, enjoying the campus, then drove into Boston to tour the John Fitzgerald Kennedy Library and Museum at the University of Massachusetts. The building is one of Boston's most dramatic architectural statements with an 135,000-square-foot library/archive, an 18,000-square-foot museum and a 20,000-square-foot center used for educational programs. The purpose of the library is to advance the study and understanding of President Kennedy's life and career, the times in which he lived and to promote a greater appreciation of America's political and cultural heritage. The museum portrays the life of President Kennedy and conveys his enthusiasm for politics and public service. Then we drove to Boston College where my dad had graduated. We found there a library named after Thomas P. (Tip) O'Neill, Jr., a Boston College alumnus and congressman from Massachusetts. Visiting a variety of college campuses intrigued us.

We stopped in Caroga Lake, New York to visit friends at their summer home who we had met at Lagoons. We went to Cooperstown together to see the Baseball Hall of Fame, a long-time dream of mine. It was quite a place. Once a year the Orioles sponsor a tournament that was held at Cooperstown. Very coincidentally, the tournament was being played the day we were there. The two teams were both in Orioles' uniforms, one in black, one in white. Some of the members had been to the Orioles fantasy camps and wore the uniform of the player they became at that camp. The players in that tournament were made up from teams in Baltimore, Washington, DC and the Virginia areas. All had to be over 30 years old to play. Some looked at least our age. There was a fantastic display about the Big Mac (Mark McGuire) and Sammy (Sosa). Everything was up to date, all the plaques and stats.

While we stayed with our friends in New York we played bridge, went swimming and water skiing. It was my first time in 30 years and I didn't do too well. Bob got up right away and stayed up and then decided not to press his luck more than once. Baggins seemed to feel very at home sitting by the lake. Bob helped them put in new kitchen cabinets, a counter top and sink. We both helped paint the kitchen. We enjoyed doing house projects wherever we went. They took us sightseeing to an unusual Russian Orthodox Church and cemetery, built in 1923 in Jordanville, New York.

We drove to Cape Cod in Massachusetts and could only get reservations in our system's campground for two nights so we made the most of the short time, taking the ferry on foot to Martha's Vineyard for dinner, and driving in the car through Hyannis to see President Kennedy's National Historic Site. It was a modest frame house, the first home shared by the president's father and mother. It represents the social and political beginnings of one of the world's most prominent families. After President Kennedy's assassination in 1963, his family repurchased the nine-room birthplace and restored it as a memorial to him. We also stopped on the beach at Provincetown at the end of the Cape near Pilgrim's Landing. The water was chilly at 62 degrees but so clear and refreshing. It was a small beach, but the first time either of us had been to Cape Cod National Seashore. In New Hampshire we stayed on a beautiful beach on a sunny day on Winnepesaukee Lake that was near Lake Squam where *On Golden Pond* was filmed.

Next we headed to the Province of Quebec in Canada. We were not thrilled at first because we ran into so many people who spoke no English. Even in India and Israel, the signs were in three languages, but in Quebec, signs were only in French. We had trouble finding the campground and ended up going right through the middle of Montreal in the motor home during rush hour as it started to rain. Bob drove from street to street while I misread the map time and time again. We were frazzled, hot, and harried by the time we arrived. A French speaking man tried to tell us something when he pulled up next to us at a light. It turned out that one of the motor home levelers had leaked oil from the broken hydraulic line. It had sprayed oil all over the car and the back of the motor home. Once we got to the campground, we immediately got back in the car, drove back into Montreal to see the Expos baseball game. Our son, John had told us the Olympic Stadium (Stade Olympique) was spectacular and it was. By the time we got to the game it was already in the sixth inning. It was too dark to get good pictures. The outside structure was incredibly huge. It had been built for the Olympics in 1976. The entire parking area and concessions were under the field. Inside there were 8,000 fans. What a shame not to have better attendance at such an innovative stadium. We enjoyed being inside in a perfectly controlled temperature for a September evening. However, we learned that the retractable roof had been inoperable ever since it was built.

After cleaning up the car a bit the next day, we crossed over into the Province of Ontario where the signs went back to English. We found a nice campground to relax in after two days of long hours of driving in the rather hot motor home. The temperature was warm enough that the air-conditioners couldn't keep up. Although we were not always able to listen to the Orioles play baseball during our travels, we did hear that Cal Ripken, an important baseball player from our hometown, had hit his 400th home run that day. We drove into Toronto, the capitol of Ontario and took an hour driving tour that we found in a magazine. We kept folders for all 50 states and Canada's provinces and whenever we read something interesting we put it in that state's folder for a time when we would be there. The tour included seeing the Royal Ontario Museum (ROM), the CN Tower (very much like the Seattle Needle) as well as the Toronto Blue Jays Skydome. We weren't able to get inside the Skydome because it was the wrong time for tours and there was no game at that time so we satisfied ourselves with pictures of the outside of the structure. We drove along Yonge Road, Route 401, which is the longest road in the world. The day before, there had been a 63-car pile up further west on the same road we traveled, but closer to Detroit in Windsor. Many were killed.

When we arrived in Sault (pronounced Soo) Saint Marie, Ontario we found a hydraulic mechanic to work on the motor home at the end of the day. Not only was his crew willing and able to work late to get us fixed. They also welded our windshield wipers that had quit during the rain in Montreal. We expected that he could charge us outrageously because of our circumstances, but the charge was incredibly reasonable which gave us a good feeling about Canadians.

We stayed in Ontario campgrounds with nice trails where I walked Baggins without a leash and we got in lots of walking exercise for both of us. One of the most interesting spots we had been to we came upon by accident. The campground was called Gitchee Gummee from the poem Hiawatha. There were many poems from Hiawatha etched in rocks, as well as sandblasted etchings on huge rocks which were then painted. John Kennedy, George Bush, Houdini, Indians, the Edmund Fitzgerald ship that sunk in Lake Superior in 1927 were the subjects of some of those etchings. We didn't figure out how the artist had picked whom to include but all around the campground were these etchings. Then just across the road was a beautiful beach right on Lake Superior. The way the sun hit the waves was breathtaking. Baggins enjoyed walking on the beach with us in the wind.

Our friends from Clinton, Michigan came up to Sault Saint Marie, Ontario to take a long train ride to Agawa Canyon with us. It was a good way to spend a rainy day. We had packed a picnic lunch and then had to eat it on the train. The minute we finished eating the sun came out just long enough for us to take an hour hike. Then the rain returned and it was time for the train to leave to go back. We had about six straight days of rain because of Hurricane Dennis, but we didn't complain because our weather for so many months had been just fantastic for whatever we were doing.

I wanted to mention the grocery shopping in Ontario. We didn't try to shop in Quebec, but in Ontario it was still an experience, even though most labels were in English as well as in French. There must not have been a law about putting nutritional information on labels there. Apparently, except for gasoline, milk, and eggs, grocery items cost less for Americans because of the devaluation of the Canadian dollar. It was the milk that intrigued us the most. Instead of being sold in a gallon jug, it was sold in bags, three bags to a package (which was another bag), the amount being about a cup more than a gallon. Everybody bought a plastic pitcher without a lid so that the small bag sat right inside the pitcher. Then it was snipped at the corner and poured from the plastic container. So the milk was left open, not capped as we were used to.

We were amazed at how huge the Province of Ontario is. We had decided to change plans a little so instead of staying in Canada to go westward, at that point, we came across the border at Sault Saint Marie into Michigan's Upper Peninsula, called the UP, to save on gasoline, both mileage wise and cost wise. We drove across Wisconsin and Minnesota and through Voyageurs National Park in International Falls, Minnesota along the border of Ontario. The topography of Voyageurs was rugged and varied, rolling hills interspersed between swamps and lakes. It held some of the world's oldest exposed rock formations.

We hit 100,000 miles on the motor home just about the time we passed the geographical center of North America in Rugby, North Dakota in mid-September. Theodore Roosevelt had many personal concerns for the environment in the North Dakota badlands even before he became the president. He was remembered with a national park named for him to honor the memory of his great conservation efforts. Among his accomplishments during his presidency was the establishment of the United States Forest Service and five national parks. The park named for him had 70,000 acres of fantastic scenery, camping and hiking. Throughout the Theodore Roosevelt National Park in Medora, North Dakota we saw bison (often called buffalo) in the road right beside the car and dozens in groups nearby the colorful rock formations. We also saw deer close beside the car. We dry camped right on the Missouri River. Dry camping is staying in your rig while not being connected to electric, water or sewer and using onboard batteries, water and holding tanks. It has the advantage of being free, usually and allowing us the freedom of camping in wilderness-type surroundings. We traveled along the Kootenai River and beside railroad tracks in Northern Montana, almost into Idaho. It reminded us of the Snake River, a beautiful sight. We stopped and took pictures of a passing train from a swinging bridge. For some distance Baggins could run free and wade in the water. During the time the East Coast was being hit by Hurricanes Dennis and Floyd, we were sitting outside in shorts on beautiful sunny days. Coincidentally, we happened to stay in the Agassiz Campground the same day that Andre Agassi won the US Open Title.

We drove across most of Montana into the northwest corner of Wyoming to see Yellowstone National Park. Yellowstone is famous for its abundant and diverse wildlife as well as for its geysers. We were fortunate enough to see a bear come right up to the car and glad that we had been instructed to keep our windows up. Yellowstone possesses close to 60 percent of the world's geysers. The Upper Geyser Basin has the largest number of geysers found in the park. There are 150 geysers within a square mile. Old Faithful is the most famous because it erupts more often than any of the other big geysers. A geyser is a spring that erupts to expel up to 8,000 gallons of boiling water at heights of up to 184 feet, an event that's amazing to watch.

Grand Tetons National Park is just south of Yellowstone, also in Western Wyoming. The Grand Teton is 13,700 feet tall in the Teton Range, an active fault-block 40 miles long with eight peaks. The park was established to protect those stunning, rugged, massive peaks as well as the diverse array of wildlife. What we saw included elk, moose, pronghorn, mule deer, bison, black bears, grizzlies, and some of the 300 species of birds, including bald eagles and peregrine falcons. Those falcons, considered endangered raptors (birds of prey) are the world's swiftest birds and are in danger of extinction in Canada and in some parts of the United States. That is why they seemed to be mentioned in many of the country's national parks.

We traveled back to the northern border of Montana for the Waterton-Glacier International Peace Park. Montana's Glacier National Park and Alberta, Canada's

Waterton Lakes National Park meet at the border between Canada and the United States. The parks were designated in 1932 to be the first International Peace Park to commemorate bonds of friendship between those two countries. We stayed at Saint Mary's Campground in Glacier National Park in West Glacier, Montana. We wanted to see the park that was established to preserve over 1 million acres of forests, meadows, and lakes that in turn provides habitats to 70 species of mammals and hundreds of bird species. Needless to say, we drove through only a small portion of the 1 million acres, marveling at the beauty. We visited my cousin in Spokane, Washington. She was disabled and lived in a group home. It was a lovely drive along the Spokane River to get there. She was surprised to see us, as she had moved, so she had not received my letter that we were coming.

When we first got into the Province of British Columbia in Canada we stayed on Christina Lake. Our motor home site was right on the sandy beach so we didn't have far to go for swimming. It got up to 86 degrees one day, although while in Canada, we had to convert the centigrade temperatures to our Fahrenheit degrees. It seemed odd going swimming while we were hearing that the temperature was 25 degrees. The Lagoons' owners from the campground in Rockport, Texas had told us that the prettiest part of Canada is in British Columbia. They gave us tips about what to see when we got there so that we wouldn't miss any of its beauty. Their brother, whom we had not previously met, took us sightseeing around Kelowna while we stayed there for three days. He worked nights so he took two days of his time off to be with us. We thought that was an extraordinary gesture of kindness. He took us to places we would not have seen if we had been on our own. We went to the tops of mountains overlooking all of Kelowna, to a spawning channel for salmon where there were walking trails, to the city park, along the Okanagan Lake, with walking and biking trails and a lock on the water which we could see close up. We walked through a tunnel and over four of the 18 trestles of an old railroad where the tracks had been taken up between the trestles to make walking easier. That was at the top of a mountain with incredible views. The part we walked took about 45 minutes each way so you can guess how long the entire walk would have been.

Coming out of Canada we drove along the North Cascade Scenic Highway to North Cascade National Park in Sedro Woolley, Washington. The park is full of mountains, valleys, waterfalls, and 700 glaciers. Ninety-eight percent of the park is wilderness, called the Stephen T. Mather Wilderness in honor of the first director of the National Park Service. Looking down into Lake Diablo, we viewed the greenest, loveliest water we had ever seen. It was very winding and took a long time to go a few miles but the drive was definitely worth it. It may have been the most magnificent scenic view at that point in our travels, glaciers in the mountains, waterfalls, so tall trees, steep grades, and colorful rock. We stopped several times to marvel at God's creations. Do not miss Route 20 on your travels. It goes through the middle of North Cascade National Park all the way to the West Coast of Washington.

We could not get tickets to the Seattle Mariners baseball game so we took a tour instead. The Safeco Field had just opened the previous July in 1999 so it was the newest at that time, very impressive. The unusual feature of that park was its retractable roof, which enabled fans to stay dry during the many rainy days that Seattle had. The roof covered the entire ballpark without enclosing it, so it had a feel of open air. It took about 15 minutes with a push of a button to open or close the roof structure that weighed 22 million pounds. Even from the center field fence, fans had a fantastic view of the baseball game. After the tour we enjoyed a ferry trip to Bainbridge Island on our way to Olympic National Park in Port Angeles, Washington. The park contains three ecosystems: glacier-capped mountains, old-growth forests, including rain forests, and the wild Pacific Coast. It is known for its biological diversity. The Olympic Peninsula, west of Puget Sound, has eight kinds of plants and 15 kinds of animals that are not found anywhere else on Earth.

Mount Rainier National Park, in Ashford, Washington includes the highest volcano in the Cascade Range, called Mount Rainier. Glaciers cover about nine percent of the total park area. Because we were there in September we could see elk that might not be seen during the other seasons. Much of the wildlife remains elusive in such wilderness that covers 97 percent of the park.

On the way to Oregon we stopped by Mount Saint Helens National Volcanic Monument that the reader may recall had nine hours of eruption on May 18, 1980. It can be seen from Spirit Lake Memorial Highway and is also in the Cascade Range. The north face of Mount Saint Helen's mountain collapsed when shaken by a 5.1

earthquake. Grey ash fell over Eastern Washington. Then President Reagan created the National Volcanic Monument for research, recreation, and education. An updated image can be viewed from the Johnston Ridge Observatory.

Just when we thought we had seen everything beautiful, on the Oregon Coast we found such fun mixed in with all the beauty. We rode in a dune buggy on 40 miles of sand dunes. It was like riding a roller coaster for a full half hour. Incredible! We wore goggles so we could see the spans of dunes while we sped along. That was so we didn't get sand in our eyes while we watched. Of course, the first time we sped down a hill and started to scream, we got sand in our mouths. So, we quickly learned to keep our mouths closed for the rest of the trip. Our guide stopped at times to explain how the dunes changed and pointed out where they were covered by water in the winter and let us take pictures. There must have been 40 state parks along the Oregon Coast and bed and breakfasts right on the water everywhere. We picked a good time of year in late September to be there because of the huge number of tourists during the summer months. It was 70 degrees and the beach was still sunny, although when we felt the water, it was very chilly.

We arrived in Crater Lake National Park in Oregon not having any idea what magnificence we were in for. Crater Lake was just like looking way down into Grand

Canyon, only filled with the bluest water you could possibly imagine. Wow! Crater Lake is known for its intense blue color. Visitors can navigate the Rim Drive around the lake, enjoy boat tours on the lake surface, or hike trails.

Next it was time to fall in love again with California. The Redwoods National Park in Orick, California was incredible. We got out and walked a trail all through the redwoods and walked along one tree that had fallen so I could estimate its height at about 200 feet. So many wows on that trip! We drove the Avenue of the Giants, too, where redwood trees stand taller than the Statue of Liberty. It is a 31-mile stretch of giant redwoods along Highway One's Pacific Coast in Northern California.

On the way to Lassen National Park we passed many, many rows of grapes growing up high off the ground, a sight we had seen in other parts of California. When we got there we took a hike. It was only 1-3/5 miles each way, but it took us a couple of hours because of the heights, up and down, and curvy. We were glad it wasn't any longer. My daily walks on flat ground were very different. The quaint college town of Davis, California where my bachelor cousin lives, is a great city for walking and bicycling. We spent some time parked in his driveway there and attended a baseball game of the Oakland Athletics at the Network Associates Coliseum in Oakland, California. That four-tiered stadium with green seats was built in a circular shape. Diamond Vision video/scoreboards were located above both the left and right field bleachers, so it was very easy to keep track of the game from any of the seats. We also attended a play in the small college town of Davis for another enjoyable evening. Often we would see signs about high school or college plays or musical presentations that were very good and admission was usually free or minimal. It was worthwhile to see the results of the efforts from teachers, students and staff.

Just outside the south gate of Yosemite, we found a very nice restaurant called the Narrow Gauge Inn and had a wonderful birthday dinner, salmon for me and steak for Bob. It was delightful, a little fancier than we normally did, with a window seat and a terrific view. It was indeed a nice 54th birthday for me. We didn't go into the Yosemite National Park because of the $20 entrance fee.

Sequoia National Park had such windy roads that I became carsick. That was the only time during our travels that had happened. After going through the Sequoia and Kings National Parks and discovering that the sequoia trees are even bigger than the redwoods, we drove down through California to Yuma, Arizona, where we found it to be 100 degrees and more. What a change in temperature that was from the Pacific Northwest. We passed the unusual vista of many, many windmills on the mountaintops. We spotted thousands of windmills on the top of mountains, erected there to provide wind energy. That is an environmentally friendly source of electricity. Wind power was starting to become popular, especially in the Palm Spring area of California. The reader could take a tour through a forest of stupendous windmills on an electric-powered vehicle, something that we did not take the time to do. Then we passed through Selma, California the raisin capital of the world.

Then we headed to Las Vegas, Nevada to spend time with our son, Loren and his daughter, Ashley. We stayed at an unusually hotel-like resort in our Coast to Coast system in Las Vegas where they had a building with a reservation desk like one would see at a fancy hotel, complete with slot machines. We paid five dollars per night for what others were paying $45 a night. We were only allowed to stay there for one week and we enjoyed every minute of it, having Ashley with us for most of that time. It was fun having her at that beautiful campground with several pools. She liked Baggins, too. While in Las Vegas we went to a very special water show to music at the Bellagio Casino. It is an astonishing sight and it is free, different music and water movements shown every 15 minutes. One could stand there for an entire evening to watch. Bellagio's also has an extraordinary garden display inside, which changes with the seasons.

Over the mountain from Las Vegas, called the "hump to Pahrump" by the locals, we stayed at the Preferred RV Resort in Pahrump, Nevada. We had stayed previously and had made some friends there. Ashley spent several nights with us there and we took her to church while she visited. She enjoyed the shuffleboard and swimming with us. She was quite a little fish. Living in a warm climate since she was two had allowed her to become a good swimmer by age seven. While in Pahrump we helped friends build a room to house their endless pool. That was a five by seven pool with a current so you could swim in one place and get a good workout. Loren, our son living in Las

Vegas, came to help us put on the roof. We also did some more work for a disabled friend whose carport needed painting after a storm had torn it down. While we were painting, Bob's ladder collapsed and suddenly he had fallen on his back and head onto the concrete. He was holding the paint can, so paint went everywhere, too. It took lots of visits to the massage therapist and to the hot tub in the park  before he felt better. We thanked God that we didn't need to get him to a hospital.

Each time we would go into Las Vegas to visit Loren and Ashley we would also make a stop at one of the casinos. The planned implosions, the violent inward collapses, started in 1993 when casino owners wanted to rebuild. So many of the casinos were very new. New York New York Casino had a roller coaster above the pool area and it went all around the buildings that made up that casino, including Coney Island and Brooklyn shops. We also met a college friend who frequently visited in-laws in Las Vegas for dinner. There was so much to do in Las Vegas, even without gambling. There were many free shows. We got to see the *Rat Pack* show which we enjoyed, as Frank Sinatra and Sammy Davis, Jr. were particular favorites of ours, although the look-alikes weren't as good as our friend Michael Hoover in his tribute to Elvis. We attended the show *Lord of the Dance*, a Celtic sort of tap dancing. We went through Tropicana Casino and won seats at two shows there, a magic show and *Follies Bergere*. We also got free tickets to an Elvis impersonator show. The Tropicana had the Las Vegas Museum for free that told its casino's history including which stars had performed there. There was a film about the fires and implosions. We used the crosswalks above those streets for getting to the MGM Grand Casino where we saw lions living there in a natural habitat. They had been raising lions there so there were many cubs. There was also a section of the casino made to resemble a rain forest and a juice bar with bar stools that looked like different animals' legs. We took the tram to Mandalay Bay, Luxor, and Excalibur Casinos. We had a Mexican lunch at The Orleans Casino and met friends from Lagoons there too. We enjoyed the inside decorations and exhibits in so many of the casinos. The outsides were exquisite and from a distance the lights at night were quite a spectacle.

We changed our Coast to Coast home-park membership from Crossville, Tennessee to Pahrump, Nevada which enabled us to stay free at Preferred RV Resort for 35 consecutive days and after that we could buy more days for six dollars per night. That was all part of our dues and with our son and granddaughter so near we decided it would be a good place to come back to each year. We shared a wonderful Thanksgiving dinner in the campground clubhouse and had a chance to help out a little, serving 136 people. It was a great meal even though we didn't know too many of the campers who were traveling through. Most of the people we had met in Pahrump from playing bridge in the previous year lived in the town, not at the campground. Many campers had returned home for the holidays.

Every morning when I walked with Baggins I also picked up litter in the desert. I organized a group at the campground to help. There was very little recycling done in Pahrump and trash was everywhere alongside the roads. It was an unincorporated town so there were not many services provided. We collected quite a stack of bagged trash and bulk trash and left it on the street for the city to pick up.

Our youngest son, Joshua came from college in Massachusetts to spend Christmas with us, arriving on December 17th. We thought it would be fun for Joshua to come there to a place he hadn't visited before. Just behind our camping site, Joshua stayed in a little park model (a small manufactured home made for RV resorts) that the campground rented for relatives and friends of campers staying in the resort. We took him to the senior center with us to play bridge and we wrapped up and took some door prizes with us. After the bridge playing, Joshua called out the winners and helped to make it more enjoyable for everyone. We had lots of fun sightseeing nearby, to China Date Ranch where one wouldn't expect to see such an oasis. The dates were picked individually from the date trees. We took Joshua into Las Vegas to see a fantastic show with Danny Gans, an impressionist. Joshua took Ashley to see a magic show we had already seen. Bob and Joshua went on the roller coaster at the Stratosphere Casino and the upside down roller coaster at the New York New York Casino where we also played games at Coney Island. We spent Christmas Eve with Loren's family, opening packages and sharing dinner, then drove back to Pahrump in time to go to Midnight Mass. Again we put our Christmas gifts on the motor home dashboard for decorations. After opening packages with Joshua the next morning, we had Christmas dinner with our Pahrump friends and their daughter from California. It was really nice spending time with both Loren and Joshua during the holidays. The weather was mostly wonderful. After the sun went down, it would get chilly and a few nights were downright cold, but during the day the sun was always out and we were able to get in lots of swimming in the outdoor-heated pool at the RV resort.

On New Year's Eve, Bob and I drove the 1-1/4 hours to Las Vegas and on the way we realized that it was midnight already on the East Coast and few of the imagined problems associated with Y2K had taken place. We found parking easily, despite what had been reported on the news stations and discovered no crowds on the Las Vegas Boulevard Strip. We went into the Luxor Casino that was the closest one to where we parked and played a nickel-slot machine slowly for about an hour. We knew that if we were gambling when they passed out champagne to everyone, we would get some. It came in very cute plastic stemware that we took outside with us at midnight. When the time came we toasted with each other and threw confetti I had brought with me on the few strangers who were also in the street. The signs said, "Happy New Year 2000" and confetti spewed from the Eiffel Tower at the Paris Casino, but that was about all the excitement in the streets, although there had been so much hype about that special turn of the century in Las Vegas. They estimated that instead of attracting 2 million people, Las Vegas had about 200,000 people come to town, the number they usually had on a slow Tuesday. Apparently everyone was scared away by hearing that everything was sold out and for big bucks way ahead of time. We felt blessed to be alive and happy to be celebrating our turn of the century in a town known for its celebrations.

"Two roads diverged in a wood,
and I - I took this one less traveled by,
and that has made all the difference."

— From *The Road Not Taken* by Robert Frost

Chapter Five

Our Third Year - Meeting Friends

Our Journey in 2000

From Nevada to Texas, Missouri to Indiana and Michigan,
From Maryland down the East Coast through Tennessee to Texas

At the beginning of our third year on the road in the new millennium, we had already seen so much of the United States, Canada, and a little of Mexico. We'd made lots of new friends and visited many old ones. We often were asked what part was our favorite. We were still seeking that answer. There seemed to be something special about each place we visited.

We left Pahrump, Nevada on January 2, 2000 after nothing had happened having to do with Y2K. We hadn't been concerned and weren't surprised. We headed for Phoenix, Arizona where we visited our Maryland friends. It was always nice to see their beautiful home with their own grapefruit and orange trees in the backyard. Baggins didn't like being left in the yard while we went out for lunch one afternoon so he chewed up the gate, which we replaced before we left town. We think Baggins had been abused before we adopted him. He would always stay near us and he liked being walked on a leash but he did not like being chained up or enclosed without us being present. In five years, we only had two problems with Baggins. The other one occurred in Michigan and is related later in this chapter.

On the way out of Arizona we took a different route that time, on Route 60, passed the Salt River Canyon, a scenic drive through the White Mountains, with a 2,000-foot-deep river canyon. It is sometimes called the mini-Grand Canyon. Route 60 winds down one wall of the canyon, crosses the Salt River at a low point over a bridge, then climbs up the other side. It is vast and wild. We found many opportunities to stop at pullouts at varying elevations on both sides of the canyon to park and enjoy the views.

In New Mexico we passed over the Continental Divide, which is 7,796 feet above sea level. Then we visited my high school friend in Lubbock, Texas. We hadn't seen each other in 18 years. After an extensive nursing career she had recently become an archeologist and visiting her was fascinating. The area was one that grew cotton and we had never seen cotton in the fields close up before. We drove through Eden, Texas on Route 83 that is the geographical center of Texas. We stayed near San Antonio one night but unfortunately the famous River Walk was being cleaned so that the river was just a mess of trash, after being drained. When we had been there before, the weather had not cooperated, but this time the weather was great, but not the river. After an eight-day trip we arrived at Lagoons RV Resort in Rockport, Texas where we had wintered the year before. It was good to get reacquainted with our old friends there, many who had helped to build the clubhouse facility during the previous winter. The owner had more projects for the Winter Texan men to do for the RV resort each year we were there. The campers made all of the picnic tables for each of the eventual 300 sites. There were advantages to staying in one place for a length of time and also to returning to the same campground year after year. Making lasting friendships was one of them. Another was being able to have a phone. It was the first time in over two years that we could give out a number to our children. They always had an emergency number in order to reach us if they had to, but they mostly depended on our calling them from a phone booth. Having a phone also made Internet access easier, so we could try to learn more about investing. We couldn't use our free Juno because there was no local access number in Rockport for Juno or for America On Line (AOL) so in addition to the phone line we signed up for an Internet server for the four months we spent in Rockport.

We took Baggins to the vet for a bath, after all the dust in Nevada and were shocked to discover he had heartworm disease, but after four weeks of rest and medicine, he felt better. I learned that he had the heartworm disease when the nurse told me and then she went on to other patients. I started crying and she came back and apologized. I had thought that heartworms were always fatal and she didn't realize that when she had walked away. I was delighted to learn that they could be treated. Baggins started getting us up every day after that at six o'clock in the morning wanting to be fed. The medicine must have affected him that way. We were glad that he would then go back to sleep until

about eight o'clock and wait for me to walk him then. He spent a lot of time up on the motor home dashboard watching and waiting for us whenever we were out and it was always a pleasant sight to come home to see him wagging his tail up on the dash.

Bob and I were workcampers that season at Lagoons. In exchange for 36 hours of combined work each week we got our site, electric, and cable television free. That helped us with our expenses. Bob worked as pool manager, while I handled the recycling like I did the year before. But that year somebody else took all the tabs off of the aluminum cans for the Ronald McDonald House so that was something I didn't need to do. Instead I did some Bible study in my extra time. I joined the campground choir, just for the rehearsals, as we went to various churches in the area on Sundays. We found out about different activities in the churches and got involved in several. We often went to Mass, including the Easter candlelight vigil that year. At the Methodist church we helped with some construction there and joined the Prime Timers, a group of older senior citizens that met for a potluck once a month. At the Presbyterian Church, we enjoyed the free dinners that preceded the pastor-led Bible study. On occasion we contributed to those dinners. At Coastal Oaks Baptist Church, we both were involved in separate Bible studies and often went to the church service there. We learned that year that Baptists did not celebrate the Season of Lent. During Lent the other area churches got together for Lenten lunches and that was where we learned about many of the varied programs. We were always on the lookout for ways to meet different people with varying interests.

We continued to play bridge and we started square dancing again. We hadn't realized how much we missed it in the couple years we had been on the road. We had purposefully joined a beginners square dancing class the year before we went on the road in order to be able to enjoy that activity across the country. Bob got the pool nice and warm, as he was able to work on it every day. Everything in the clubhouse looked good. That was what Bob had spent most of his time working on in the previous year. It was the biggest clubhouse we had seen and there were lots of activities always going on. We had to make choices as to what to attend because there was more to do than we had time for. We had a potato dinner there one night for a dollar with all kinds of fixings to go on huge baked potatoes. They were right about things being bigger in Texas! Then Bob won $13 on a 50/50 drawing. That is when a person buys a ticket for a dollar or so and after all the money is collected, a ticket is drawn and the winner gets half the pot while the other half goes to a charity. Volunteers baked 40 pies for a craft and rummage sale in the clubhouse. They sold pieces for one dollar and sold every pie.

That night we had a talent show that was hysterical. It was so funny and so well done. The clubhouse was packed with almost everybody from the 250 sites in attendance. There were so many cute skits. A night of laughter was always good medicine. And we got a different perspective on some of the people we thought we knew!

The weather was good in January. We had many days in the 80s and beginning in February, we had more good weather. For Valentine's Day there was a dinner and dance at the clubhouse. The men did the cooking on a grill and served the ladies. It was good to have a friend who also had a dog and was willing to watch Baggins for us when we spent all day and evening going to Mexico for dental work. About 30 rigs (RVs) left the campground on March first but 10 more came in. Campers had begun to leave for home or for other warmer parts of the country. For three months just about all 250 spaces were occupied. That was the way it was for many of the campgrounds in the warmer parts of the United States and Mexico during the winter months. Those who traveled from the north to Texas were affectionately called Winter Texans while those who traveled to Florida and Arizona were called Snowbirds. Some of those campers were full-time RVers and others were traveling back and forth to their northern homes.

We had almost no rain, except for one day in late March when we got at least eight inches at one time and the campground flooded. That was a mess with lots of things floating through the water. We had shoes and coolers flow into our site and had to find their owners. We didn't keep anything outside under our motor home so we didn't lose anything. It was kind of fun looking for owners of lost clothing. In general, however, the weather was just wonderful for the four months we were at Lagoons RV Resort.

By April, more than half of the campers had left. By May only about 20 were still there although some people left their rigs stored on their site. About 15 of the people who remained lived there all year long. It was kind of fun being there without all the others. Without the rigs in the park, we could see the clubhouse and it looked a lot closer than it had. It wasn't considered friendly to walk through another person's site. After so many rigs were gone, we could cut right through by walking or riding bikes. Baggins had a chance to walk all around unleashed which he couldn't do when the park was full. We had spent many hours walking around the pond behind the campground in the woods, a nice spot for morning walks. That spring there were two horses behind the fence when we walked. Many times we saw egrets, wild boars and the same rosetta spoonbill, an unusual bird. Rockport and the Aransas area is a great birding spot where people come from all over the world to view birds. Some birders keep life lists to keep track of which birds they had seen, maybe only once in their lives. There are two places in the southern part of the United States that attract the migratory whooping cranes. We had the opportunity to see them in the Rockport-Fulton area, an international birding spot for whooping cranes, passerines, waterfowl, raptors and 500 other species. Whooping cranes nest in Canada during the summer and migrate to that area for the winter.

Snakes started to come out in May when it got hotter, so it suited me to walk around the concrete areas in our last month there. Mosquitoes came and went. It depended on the wind. We had lots of nice breezes even when the sun was really hot. After the Texas red ants bit my feet, I did most of my walking in the pool, which was the only time when my feet didn't itch. I learned not to wear open sandals and to pay special attention to where I was walking. We took Baggins to the beach often enough that he seemed to enjoy the swimming. Prior to that he liked to wade, but the first time at the beach, I had to drag him out to where he had to swim. He panicked a little, but did just fine once we went a few times. Bob and I got badly sunburned our first time out.

We didn't do much sightseeing while at Lagoons that year, but we did attend a wonderful Passion play and listened to a wonderful speaker, Darrell Scott, the father of one of the murdered children from Columbine High School in Colorado. He gave up his good job to go around the country giving very spiritual talks. We were glad we had heard about that. We also went to an adult Easter egg hunt after church on Easter with a picnic afterwards, hosted by a local square dancer. We attended a HFHI ceremony in Rockport. The affiliate had just gotten started the past year and they dedicated the ground for the first house.

The third time was the charm. Our first stop when we left Lagoons was the River Walk in San Antonio for lunch. The two other times we had visited the River Walk were not pleasant times, because of excessive heat and the draining of the river, so we really enjoyed sitting outside for lunch next to the river. It was just perfect that third time. While visiting a Lagoons friend in Lago Vista, Texas, near Austin, we saw so many deer lying on people's lawns that they seemed to be tame. Amazing! It was in Austin that we toured the Lyndon Baines Johnson Library and Ranch. It turned out to be my favorite. We actually got to see Mrs. Johnson as she was being driven into her driveway. Bob had previously met both of the Johnsons when he was working for the Social Security Administration in their new building in Baltimore, Maryland. He took both of them on a tour of the building during Mr. Johnson's presidency.

Bob visited the George Bush Library in College Station, Texas. The exhibit at the Bush Museum traced the life of President George H. W. Bush from his childhood during the 1920s through his service as a fighter pilot during World War II and his business career spanning the decades between 1945 and 1965. It continued with his political career. We took several days to travel from there to Branson, Missouri so that we didn't have to drive too long each day and could relax in the afternoons. It was a leisurely time and felt good after all the activity at Lagoons.

We spent the next few days in hot, green, beautiful Southern Missouri. What a place! It was an area we hadn't been before. We met friends at Lagoons who had a home in Branson on Table Rock Lake, which is a man-made lake about 80 miles around. The road around the lake seemed to go on forever, winding all around, and made driving in that area so beautiful no matter where we were going. Years ago, sometime in the 1950s, they actually made a dam and then flooded over houses and a bridge. First they had to put up the new bridge. The area was all under about 200 feet of water, just incredible. When we arrived, we put our motor home on a pad about 10 minutes from their house. Our friend owned a lot with a building on it for storing his motor home and he had added pads with full hookups for visitors and friends with motor homes. Once we started RVing, we met lots of people who also RV. If you have a house, it is nice to have a place for your RV friends to hookup their RV if they wanted to stay in their motor home instead of in the house. We discovered that friends who weren't familiar with the RV lifestyle didn't understand why we would rather stay in our motor home when we visited them. It had everything we needed right there without having to pack. Our bed was very comfortable. We had all the conveniences of a home and our RV did feel very much like home to us. We also understood that not everyone is as fond of dogs as we are.

That evening we all went to see a Chinese Acrobatic show. Because they lived in the popular area of Branson, the shows gave free tickets to them for the inconvenience of having to put up with traffic and they had guest passes for us, too. It was a marvelous show. You can't imagine the number of ways those performers could twist their bodies. The strength it took in their arms especially was overwhelming. The next day our friends also had extra passes for Silver Dollar City, a cross between an amusement park with wet rides (with all the extra shows during that month being musical-type shows) and an old-fashioned park set in the 1800s. We got to see candlemaking, horseshoeing, blacksmithing, and a comedy show at the saloon. Silver Dollar City was an all-day event and we had perfect weather for it. Then we had dinner at a restaurant called Top of the Rock that had an unbelievable view of Table Rock Lake.

Following that, we spent five hours of the next afternoon on their boat, riding around the lake, and anchoring to swim and sunbathe, another perfect weather day in the 90s and sunny. We found them to be very good company and appreciated so much that they had invited us to spend time in Branson. We had only heard about its country music and found it to be much, much more. Branson had more theatres for shows than New York City, something we hadn't known. It was glitzy, like Las Vegas but we didn't do much of that sort. Instead, we took advantage of the gorgeous weather. We felt truly blessed that a couple we hardly knew treated us to a wonderful visit in such a friendly, welcoming manner. We drove from there to Carthage, Missouri to stop at the Precious Moments Chapel Center. We were familiar with the Precious Moments figurines, but had no idea they were conceived by an artist, Sam Butcher who decided at a young age that he was going to dedicate his life to Jesus. He started painting the Precious Moment figures and a company talked him into letting them make the drawings into figurines, and the rest is history, as they say! In 1989, he began work on a chapel and did all the painting by himself. He spent over two years on his back doing the ceiling, then painted several murals for the walls. It was unbelievably incredible, a part of God's Kingdom for sure. It was a place we would definitely recommend. He had a room off the main chapel dedicated to the memory of his son who died at age 27, leaving a wife and three children behind. He even put Precious Moments on tombstones for people who requested that. What a spiritual experience it was. Many children who had died had become the special angels in the murals, especially the huge one called Hallelujah Square. All of his Precious Moments figurines were displayed in another building and it was hard to believe he had time to do all that he did in his lifetime. He was 61 years old and expected to keep at it. We wanted to get back there some day to see his changes and feel the spirituality again. We were grateful to the person who suggested we go there.

Next we went to a campground in Blue Springs, Missouri with the beach that joined the pool water where we stayed two years ago in July. It had amazed us then and it amazed us again that time. It was the only one like it we had ever seen. The Harry S. Truman Library was in Independence, Missouri. Highlighted at the Truman Library are major issues and events of Harry Truman's presidency in a 10,500-square-foot-core exhibition. There are many special collections that have special historical or artistic value.

We continued in a northeasterly direction to see the Lincoln Memorial in Springfield, Illinois. We found it in Oak Ridge Cemetery. The memorial is the actual burial place of Abraham Lincoln's body. His wife and three of their children are also buried there. Mary Todd and Abraham Lincoln had had four boys. The oldest, Robert Todd Lincoln, lived to be 83 years old. Edward died at the age of four. Willie died at age 11. Tad died at age 18. The most popular part of the memorial is the bust of Lincoln out in front. Within the memorial are many various original or miniature representations of statues of Lincoln from around the United States. In the Oak Ridge Cemetery was also an awesome Viet Nam Veterans Memorial. It was built in 1988 in a circular design with no beginning and no end, much like a wheel with the spokes being walls for each branch of the service and a list of POW/MIAs. We looked over the five grey granite walls with the names of veterans from Illinois who died or are still missing from the Viet Nam War. An eternal flame is on top of the walls where they meet in the center. It was very impressive.

We visited the Saint Louis Cardinals Busch Stadium. Before we went inside we saw statues of famous players on the Plaza of Champions. Inside it had a grass field, bullpens behind the outfield fence, and a huge manual scoreboard. The four tiers of red seats were the same color as the Cardinals uniforms. At the Anheuser/Busch Budweiser Brewery, we took a tour, and then stopped in South Bend, Indiana.

We were honored when we arrived in South Bend. A very prominent architect, LeRoy Troyer, invited four other couples to join us for dinner because we were in town. LeRoy was the house leader for President Carter every year at the JCWP. Three of the four other couples had worked with us on the Carter Youth Center in April 1999. Two of them were from LeRoy's office and he had sent them down there to help out. The other was his brother, whom we'd met before, on that build and on the Houston build. The other couple was Art Moser & his wife. Bob had been on LeRoy's house in Houston when President Carter had asked him to help out at the Notre Dame student house where Art was house leader. Bob had been glad to do that as he was a Notre Dame graduate in 1967 and he enjoyed meeting and working with some of the current students. (When we mention that a Habitat house is the Notre Dame house or the Dow house or the house of a church, it means that those named organizations sponsor the house either with funds, volunteers or both.) Then we also saw Art last year at the South Bend build. We ended up parking our motor home in the Mosers' driveway while we visited in South Bend. Bob wanted to meet with the Habitat director to see what he needed to get together for our return to the Notre Dame alumni blitz build the following week.

We toured LeRoy's office and found a very interesting plaque hanging there. It was a statement of all the office's Christian policies. There was also a wall full of pictures of the entire families of every employee. LeRoy was an extraordinary person and apparently so were the people who worked for him. In the summer he paid college students to intern there to learn more about architecture. LeRoy graduated from Notre Dame in 1971, so he was there at least one year that Bob was there, but he told us that he was 33 years old at the time. He was involved in so many projects that it was mind-boggling. He was hardly ever home and seemed genuinely pleased that he was in town when we arrived. He was going to Europe the next day so he wasn't there that year for the Notre Dame build in South Bend. He had visited the site the year before. Recently, he had been working in Nazareth, Israel on a project where Phase One was opened in June of 2000 with people stationed along the trip up the mountain, telling about the parables of Jesus. To hear him talk was a neat experience because LeRoy was so excited when he talked about Jesus and being able to work in the same area where Jesus and Joseph probably worked. They uncovered some things that they think Jesus worked on. It sounded very interesting. While nearby, in Elkhart County, the largest motor home manufacturing area in the world, we toured the Holiday Rambler factory in Wakarusa, Indiana.

We stopped at another Lagoons friend's home in Gaines, Michigan for a day's visit on our way to see college friends, Dave and Mary, in Clinton, Michigan to help them with their daughter's wedding. As soon as we got there, they put us right to work. Getting ready for an outdoor wedding on 80

acres took a lot of mowing, weeding, painting, and setting up. I painted four foot by eight foot sheets of plywood with "Lazor-Smith Wedding" and parking information that were put on the main road to direct guests. I helped Mary with table centerpieces. Dave and Bob worked on siding one side of a barn. There were eight big buildings on the property and that was one that hadn't been completed because of all the rain. One hundred twenty-five guests were expected. A huge tent was put up and the weather for the wedding day was perfect, despite all the rain that had recently been received in that area. While the wedding day proceeded, Bob and I kept the bartender and caterers and band members organized so the wedding party and parents could just enjoy themselves. The square dance caller was terrific and a lot of people joined in the Virginia Reel and square dancing-type dances. After the band left, the bride's brothers and cousin orchestrated about 40 minutes of fireworks that were fantastic. Then a huge bonfire was lit and it wasn't until after midnight that the rains started again. It didn't keep people from sitting out under the cabana area near the bonfire. There were cameras on all 25 tables for everyone's use, and as I noticed they were not being used, I made sure all the pictures got taken. It was a smashing, unique wedding and we had lots and lots of fun being part of it.

The following day we left for South Bend to begin building Tamika's Habitat house. We arrived with the decking for the floor already completed including a

stairway installed for the basement entry. For a blitz build when a Habitat house got finished in one week, the local crew and partner families had already gotten the house to that point before the week began. By Friday the house was complete, even the landscaping. We worked with most of the people who came the year before and had a great build week, especially with Father Jim from Notre Dame there to say Mass every day and with the terrific meals at Notre Dame's South Dining Hall. Bob was again the house leader, getting everybody organized for the job each particularly liked. Mostly I kept everybody in water and sunscreen but I got to work on the shingles for two days and enjoyed that a lot.

After the blessing of the house on Friday we stayed a few days to visit the campus and catch up with a couple friends from Lagoons who happen to live in South Bend during the summer months. Then we went back to Michigan where we had left the motor home while we stayed in the dorm at Notre Dame. During that time we had left Baggins at Mary and Dave's where he slept in the motor home at night. After waiting for us for seven days, Baggins had had enough of being left by us and made quite a mess in the motor home which Mary had to clean up on two mornings. We learned another lesson about Baggins and hoped that Mary would forgive us. Then we went to the new Detroit Tigers Comerica Park with them. It was a sold-out game against the Yankees with the cheapest seats being eight dollars. They let us in with standing-room-only tickets at $15 each. Outrageous! But one more stadium was added to our list. As we entered Comerica Park, we were greeted by a 25-foot by 15-foot tiger made of concrete. That park was just a mile from the old Tiger Stadium, but it was very different, with three levels of seats and no obstructions. Most of the seats had a good view of downtown Detroit. The bullpens were behind the right-field wall. In center field were located several fountains that produced liquid fireworks when a home run was hit. A huge scoreboard sat behind left field. Much like Oriole Park at Camden Yards in Baltimore, Maryland the playing surface was 25 feet below street level. There was a Ferris wheel and a merry-go-round at the park.

The Saint Joseph County Habitat director talked us into coming back to South Bend so that Bob could lead a crew to put decking on five more houses so that they would be ready for other groups to complete during that summer. So we stayed at his house on Lake Michigan, very nice water, no seaweed or sea nettles, unlike the parts of the Atlantic Ocean in Maryland and New Jersey that we were used to swimming in, and Baggins got to go in it. I walked their dog, a big golden retriever, on her leash and Baggins ran along with us. I think I wore out both dogs. Bob worked in South Bend, about an hour from there. The time change was weird. He left Union Pier, Michigan at eight o'clock in the morning and got to South Bend, Indiana at eight o'clock in the morning! When I wasn't dog-sitting, we drove down together. One day I sorted nails, cleaned out and organized materials and tool trailers; then another lady volunteer and I nailed all the plywood down to make the floor of the house while Bob's crew put in all the joists on another house. They also had to put in stairs to the basement. Then the houses would be ready for a blitz build by some other group. He and the local volunteers got four of the five finished before we left. Rain kept us from completing all five but Habitat needed Bob to lead because the regular construction manager was on vacation. Each day after working in South Bend when we got back to the beach house, all we had to do was walk down from the backyard about a million steps and there was the beach! It wasn't the ocean, but it was great. There weren't many waves, so swimming was easy. Bob and I played ball in the water for a long time and it was a nice way to spend Independence Day. The director's wife was away the week we spent there, so while he went to visit her on the Fourth, we had the place to ourselves. It seemed odd to spend the Fourth of July alone, but we did get to see fireworks on the beach being displayed by others who lived nearby.

When we left Union Pier, Michigan and South Bend, Indiana we headed for Cleveland, Ohio and the Rock and Roll Hall of Fame. It had been designed to be spectacular. It was composed of bold geometric forms with a 162-foot-high tower and 150,000 square feet of exhibit space that tried to express the raw power of rock's living heritage and enduring impact on global culture. The building rises above the shore of Lake Erie as the centerpiece of Cleveland's North Coast Harbor. Then we went to The Jake. They had a #414 in red up top where everybody at the games could see it to show that they had been sold out for all their baseball games since they opened Jacobs Field for the Cleveland Indians in 1996. Along with all the names of the Cleveland players who had been retired, they also had Jackie Robinson's #42, as did all of the ballparks around the country. That was a neat park. The lights were up and down to look like the smokestacks around the city. The roof supports over the upper deck were made to resemble the bridges around the city. We took a tour because they weren't playing the day before the All-Star game and we probably couldn't have gotten tickets there anyway. We got to sit in the dugout. They had more luxury-box seats than any other stadium at that time. They called their standing-room-only section the Pepsi Home Run Plaza so it sounded like it was an honor to be standing up to watch. They did get a lot of home runs there in that section. We had a nice lunch in the Terrace Club that we were allowed to do because there was no game going on. They were opened for lunch every day just like at Camden Yards in Baltimore, Maryland our hometown.

We only had time to pass by the outside of the Pittsburgh Three Rivers Stadium because our timing didn't work out when we went to see Bob's aunts. We had friends who had a time-share at a campground on the shore in Southern New Jersey at Outdoor World Lake and Shore Resort and they let us use it since they don't have a motor home.

That was how we relaxed in New Jersey. The night we got there Bob had to go to the emergency room because of lots of pain from a pulled muscle which caused a pinched nerve. He probably overdid it at Habitat. It was great that when we got into town our son, John came over to the campground as soon as we got in and had time to sit with us at the hospital, so we had a nice, unexpected visit with him. While at the Jersey shore, we got to see five of our six children, so that was a real plus for being in the area. We had a whole week with our granddaughter Ashley besides. A seven year old takes time and lots of undivided attention and it was really nice to be able to spend the time with her and also with our friends who have the time-share. That was a family-type campground and included a huge pool and a lake for swimming. It also had an indoor water park with all kinds of slides. There were also paddleboats and many activities for the children and young adults as well as walking paths through the woods and around the lake. That was a different kind of camping for us because at our winter resort the activities were geared to senior adults. Atlantic City, New Jersey and the Atlantic Ocean were very close by so we took advantage of sunbathing, reading and swimming there.

A really funny thing happened when we took our youngest son, Joshua to the Philadelphia Airport to get him back to college in Massachusetts. We thought it would be a good chance to spend some time together, so we left for the airport early to have plenty of time for dinner --- wrong! All flights to Boston were canceled when we got there even though Joshua had called the airport to make sure everything was on time. He had not been able to get out of Boston on the previous Friday night because all flights were canceled then. Because he had to be back for work on Monday morning we quickly took him to the train station and there was a train leaving right away that we got him on, which canceled out any time we had to spend with him. Joshua got a cab with two other passengers once he got into Boston. Joshua sat in front and had to keep waking the cab driver up every time they would stop at a light. When the other two passengers got out, the cab driver told Joshua that he would have to do the driving if he wanted to get back to school, which was about another hour away. He still charged him $50 even though Joshua drove. Life is full of unforeseen pleasures as well as odd happenings.

After leaving New Jersey and stopping for our yearly physicals in Maryland, they said the weather for the weekend was supposed to be great. On the way to

Williamsburg, Virginia Bob said it was the worst storm we had ever driven in with the motor home. He had to pull off twice and used the outdoor mirror defroster for the first time. The rain stopped as we pulled in but it was still very windy. While I was outside directing Bob into the site a huge branch fell just behind me. I felt lucky that it had missed me! We got to tour the streets of Williamsburg without cost and it was nice but didn't command the hype it got on the East Coast, in our opinion. We were glad we had chosen not to purchase a ticket to tour. Instead we walked down the streets and looked into the storefronts without going inside. Maybe we had just been spoiled to have already seen so many other similar communities. At the campground we took a canoe ride on the Chickahominy River.

We loved Virginia Beach and fortunately had planned to stay there three nights, longer than any of our other stops going down the coast. The water was so much clearer than at the Jersey Shore, no seaweed or sea nettles. We spent a lot of time at the beach there. We liked the campground that had big, grassy sites, three pools and friendly people and we realized that we would consider workcamping there in the future. We went on to North Carolina where we took three different ferries. They have quite a nice free ferry system along the coast of North Carolina. We stayed near Cape Hatteras and our campsite there was actually on the ocean. We got in late in the afternoon and left the next morning, so being so close was definitely an advantage, as we had only a couple of hours for the beach. That campground normally charged $50 per night, but in our Coast to Coast system we paid our usual six dollars. We stayed overnight at Myrtle Beach, South Carolina and had a huge storm blow up after we'd been on the beach for five minutes, but that was okay, as Myrtle Beach didn't seem as nice as the others anyhow. Then we drove to Southern South Carolina and visited friends who lived on Hilton Head Island. They took us to the beautiful beach there with the water even warmer, and also took us on a tour of Savannah, Georgia that is close by. We got to take the midnight tour and later watched the movie *In the Midnight Garden of Good and Evil* set in Savannah. We also saw the spot where Tom Hanks sat on a bench waiting for a bus in the movie *Forest Gump*. Although Bob and I both had lived on the East Coast for most of our lives we had never taken the time before that to travel to those delightful southern cities and coastal beaches.

We arrived in Americus, Georgia in mid-August to participate in a JCWP Habitat blitz build. There was much preparation that went into such a build years before it started. The few weeks before the build, called the pre-build, were hectic ones and ones in which we liked to lend a hand when we had extra time. Most of the volunteers who came for the build only had a week's vacation. It was over 100 degrees when we arrived so Bob was glad his body would have an opportunity to adjust to the heat before the actual blitz build took place. Bob worked outside in that heat the first couple of days and it was difficult for his body to adjust. Then he was put inside the warehouse to supervise the loading of trailers so that was much better. Although it was just as hot in the warehouse, the sun was not beating down on him. I was on the recycling and waste management team and there wasn't much work for me during the pre-build. There were a few meetings but recycling couldn't be started until the houses were being built and there was something to recycle. With 35 houses and thousands of volunteers there that week, there was lots of waste and recyclables.

It was very interesting and enjoyable, as usual, to meet so many diverse people, all there to help out, each paying $250 for the privilege of volunteering on a JCWP (Jimmy Carter Work Project) build. During that one week, President and Mrs. Carter worked in New York City (where they did their very first build for Habitat about 14 years before), gave encouragement in Jacksonville, Florida one day where 100 houses were built that same week and then finished up the week in Plains, Georgia, Jimmy Carter's hometown, just outside of Americus, where five houses were built. Thirty houses were put up in Americus that week with President Carter presiding over all of the 35 house dedications at the end of the week. There were people from all over the world that week in September. Many readers may mistakenly think that it was the Carters who began Habitat for Humanity International. However, it had been in operation by its founders, Millard and Linda Fuller, since 1976 before they got the Carters involved eight years later. Every year after that, President Carter and his wife Rosalynn graciously gave a week of their time helping to build a Habitat house, and their doing so created much publicity for the organization. President Carter's favorite job was building porch railings.

Making friends all along the way was truly a gift for a lifetime and we thanked God every day that He had blessed us so. It was because of God's intercession that

Habitat was able to do so much in 62 countries of the world at that time. Each year the number of countries involved increased. Millard and Linda Fuller were such selfless people and so easy to be with. Their faith showed and encouraged others to have such faith. We attended President Carter's Sunday School class during that weekend and found him once again to be an unusually good speaker. He had a wonderful message for all the visitors who came to his class from around the world. Whenever he was in town, he taught. He had accomplished so much good since his presidency.

The week before 2,000 volunteers were due in Americus, Bob had been responsible for getting all the recycling signs our team had made and laminated with clear tape put up. He had found pallets to place at each house for the various types of recycled materials to be put on for easier removal from the site. I met with the Green Team, part of the volunteer effort to protect the environment by building more efficient houses to use less fuel for heating and cooling and I talked to them about recycling to get them to promote the spirit of cooperation within each house. Some people were gung ho about recycling and others could have cared less.

On Friday while Bob was meeting with other house leaders I went to registration and sat for four hours talking with people and getting some to commit to recycling at the house they would work on during the build. It was fun meeting people who had never built for Habitat before and also seeing a surprising number of people we already knew from previous builds. A girl came up to me and asked if I lived in Rockport. I said, "Well sort of, in the winter". She worked with my Sunday school teacher from Rockport, and he had asked her to look us up. She told him he was crazy, that there would be thousands of people there and yet she spotted my nametag! Nametags were required of all volunteers because of security during a Carter build. Some people were staying with local families. Some were staying on the floor of churches, some in motels. The year before, people stayed in the dorms of the local colleges, but late August was the wrong time of year for that. Everyone needed to be registered to find out where he/she was staying and who he/she would meet with to get started on his/her particular house.

Bob's meeting with all the house leaders was disastrous. They were gathered under the big food tent and with all the rain we had, the ground under the tent was so very wet that while they were trying to meet, a crew was trying to put straw down. The straw drew more of the already bad gnats and one girl got her hands full of fire ants that she didn't know were inside the straw. Then we went to dinner and the lines were unbelievably long. Just as we got up to the food, they ran out. All of the volunteers remained very patient. It was just that kind of group. We finally gave up on spaghetti and put sauce over bread. Then there was a beautiful rendition of the *Lord's Prayer* in song, a few words we couldn't hear and the house leaders met briefly with their members. It was chaotic, but we had lots of fun, and I recruited someone from about 32 of the 35 houses to help with recycling. When I got back to our site, one of the volunteer wives who was not participating in the build offered to walk Baggins while Bob and I worked each day and that meant a lot, not having to come back to the site during the work day. That way she felt like she was helping out while her husband was also a house leader.

By Friday night (actually Saturday at about four in the morning), I realized that the first few days of a blitz build was the week I pushed my body to its limits. I didn't know I could and then kept going after that. Saturday was a long day, after three hours sleep. Guess it was the expectations that kept me awake. We got to the site at seven o'clock for devotions, standing in the food tent, like every morning. But very thankfully we hadn't had any rain since early Friday. Things were fairly dried out except under the tent. The straw that had been put down brought with it millions of gnats and that made eating very unpleasant although the meals were really good. We gulped it down so we could get out of the tent. Some people brought dryer sheets (such as Bounce) to put under their caps that really did keep the gnats away for a while. We didn't know who came up with such an idea, but it was a blessing by the middle of the week. I stepped in fire ants first thing Saturday, while cleaning up trash in tall grass. Before we realized it, they were all over my legs, biting hard. They were what kept me up at night. The itching was unbelievable. Bob had those two weeks ago. They were weird. They made blisters and then pus came out. When that happened, they stopped itching so much. We were too busy during the day to notice the itching so much, but at night it would be all I seemed to be able to think about.

On Saturday Bob got his house up, roof covered with tar paper and he was on schedule. He had a lot of experienced help. And I found a woman to go with me in the rented pickup and the two of us went from house to house making sure every house had a garbage can, a box for aluminum cans, plastic bottles, pallets to collect shingles, drywall, and cardboard, stakes with signs to put out vinyl siding and untreated wood for mulch. The rest went into trash bags. So we spent the entire day driving around and around, picking up, loading the truck, and then unloading it. When stuff was too heavy we begged someone to help us. It usually worked, although the guys were much too interested in actually building to think about the recycling and waste phase. In and out of the truck, in and out, in and out. It got easier when the other lady drove because then the seat didn't have to be so far up and it was easier for me to get out on the passenger's side. I'm very short.

Sunday wasn't a scheduled workday so Bob and I had time to get the sites all ready for pick ups during the next week. Some pallets and signs and garbage cans had disappeared since we had first put them out and we wanted every house to be able to start out on the same footing on Monday, the first day of the full blitz week. We intended to go out for a couple of hours and ended up spending six. There were enough people working on their houses that the Habitat affiliate had dinner for us. The instructions were that the house had to be under cover with tar paper by Monday morning so anyone not finished on Saturday by dark had to come back Sunday. Bob was finished but he wanted to help me, so that worked out nicely. We ordered 400 clear bags for the cans and 400 black bags for trash and we ended up needing four times that many.

The heat was a problem. By about two o'clock each afternoon I was putting ice inside my hat that seemed to get me through. Two new women friends drove a very old, very beat up truck all week collecting cardboard, cans and bottles, untreated wood, leftover drywall, broken shingles, all to be recycled, plus general trash of all kinds while I collected in the other truck we had rented. We both got different people on different days to help us. The women were wonderful and on Thursday night we took them and two of the guys who gave up a lot of their hammering time to help the ladies with recycling and trash, out to dinner for Mexican food instead of eating in the tent full of gnats. The Aluminum Association who was in partnership with Habitat to recycle aluminum cans sponsored Bob's Habitat house. It would be too lengthy to include all that happened during the week, but hope you enjoy the highlights and get a little feel for what volunteering for HFHI means to us. Maybe some of our readers will want to find out for themselves. The conditions we worked under weren't always ideal. However, the people we worked with were all there to do God's work and the way everyone got along was a huge blessing to us.

We got to see the Carters and the Fullers for about 30 seconds on Friday afternoon when they came by to congratulate the homeowners, turn over the house keys and get a picture with our entire group, about 35 volunteers, some with the Aluminum Association, some with Alcoa, and others, like us, from different parts of the country. A good number of them had been on previous JCWP builds. By the way, it never rained the entire work-week, so God must have been with us wanting us to get all those houses finished. We were convinced that HFHI is certainly a part of the work in God's Kingdom. The partner families were incredibly grateful and showed their appreciation in various ways.

In addition to the volunteers celebrating with the homeowners the culmination of a week's work at each individual house, we attended a closing Habitation ceremony on Friday at a local school stadium. That was a usual part of the JCWP and it was moving, as always. To have heard the founder talk about his ideas and plans, many of which had already come to fruition, was stimulating. To have listened to President Carter speak about his involvement was awesome. To learn from some of the homeowners of the Habitat houses how God played such an important part in the process was inspiring. Amy Grant and the Anointed sang. The mayor of Americus and others spoke and the main speaker was a preacher from New York City. He was very good. We learned that since the last time we heard Millard speak, Habitat had gone from being in 62 countries to being in 68 countries. From building 33 houses in a month when it first started, it was building 33 houses each day. Ten thousand houses were started, finished or being worked on during that week.

There were two big reasons for celebration that week, in addition to the blitz build. HFHI had completed the building of their 100,000th house since its beginning in 1976. The second reason for an especially big celebration that year was that in 1992 Millard Fuller stood on the table in the board room to get his point across that he believed that sub-standard housing could be eliminated in Sumter County, Georgia within eight years. The members were skeptical but he said that with God all things were possible, and God gave him what he needed, because as of the date of that speech, eight years later, sub-standard housing had been eliminated in Sumter County. Being the humble man that Carter is, he said that because of him being elected president 24 years before, that was what Sumter County had been known for. Now, he said, Sumter County would forget that and be known for being the first county in the world to eliminate sub-standard housing. That was an encouragement to affiliates around the world to plan to do the same. It was also fantastic support to volunteers and contributors to continue their work. For some reason, during that ceremony at the stadium, we didn't have to fight gnats. With that alone we felt God's presence.

Being able to give a family their own home, that they had worked for and would pay for, knowing that they would take pride in it, was what made all of us able to withstand the heat, gnats, bruises, injuries and other circumstances involved in volunteering for HFHI. People that were new to working at Habitat that year, who had been pushed into volunteering by their company, couldn't believe what a good feeling it was at the end of the week to see our homeowners and their four children crying in happiness and to be a part of the spirit of giving that abounds during those builds. It was surely God's amazing grace.

Our next stop was to visit friends we had met at Lagoons who live in Tennessee. That time we left our motor home in Tennessee and drove in our car to the wedding of Bob's sister's son because we could stay with college friends in the Chicago, Illinois area and wouldn't have to put that mileage on the motor home. It was a big extravaganza and we got to be part of the 10 relatives from his nephew's side of the family. On the following day Bob and I went to see Wrigley Field while the Chicago Cubs played the Saint Louis Cardinals. We took the train and buses about two hours each way, so that was an adventure in itself. We'd heard that parking was at least $20 and that the cars were sandwiched in so if we wanted to leave the game early, driving the car was not the way to go. We had hoped to see Sammy Sosa and Mark McGuire, but they weren't playing. Instead we got to see Will Clark, a Saint Louis Cardinal, hit a grand slam! Pretty neat, eh? The back wall was covered with vines and the fans sitting nearby assured us that the vines covered bricks, so that by itself told us that Wrigley was an old field, not a good wall for a fielder to be running into. There was no Jumbotron and the scoreboard was still being changed manually by people behind it. It was a pretty field, a good part of that due to the fact that there were no advertisements on the walls. The ushers had to sit down on little collapsible seats during the innings and could only get up between innings, so that they would not be in anybody's way. Apparently the Cubs and Cardinals have a rivalry similar to that of the Orioles and the Yankees. More than half the stadium was filled with Cardinal fans, not Cub fans. We could tell when Clark hit the grand slam. The funny thing on the scoreboard showing other major league scores and pitchers' numbers was that they had #8 (Cal Ripken) pitching for the Orioles! We knew that was a mistake! For readers who may not be baseball fans, Cal Ripken was one of the greater players, but definitely not a pitcher.

We left early Wednesday morning to go back to Tennessee, a 13-hour drive which we broke up by stopping in Cincinnati, Ohio to see the Reds stadium but we couldn't get too close, as they were tearing it down already, getting ready to build a new stadium to be ready by 2003. That was one we had to put in our plans to see at a later date. As we drove through Cincinnati we saw statues of painted pigs on every corner. We inquired of several city residents why there were pigs everywhere and we learned that Cincinnati had been a hog-butchery and meat-packing center in the early 19th century. Slaughterhouses were plentiful. A Flying Pig Marathon was founded in 1988 to pay tribute to part of the city's history. Cincinnati decided to show off the city's heritage with the Big Pig Gig, strategically placing creatively decorated large plastic pigs along the route of the Flying Pig Marathon. In 2000 the plastic pigs were auctioned to support charities. Owners donated the pigs to hospitals and schools, and some sat on city corners.

We got back to our motor home and to our friends in Greeneville, Tennessee and drove with them to Chesnee, South Carolina to a bluegrass festival. There was a lot of jamming and eating on Friday night, but the big deal was Saturday night with four bands. There were about 30 recreational vehicles there, lots of people, lots of food and drink, motor homes on the lawn of the house where it was being held and on the lawns of their two neighbors. Only in America! They had put up a tent in the back yard, and had a pavilion standing all the time. They were all real friendly people, real hospitable

Southerners, and encouraged us to come back year after year. It was a different experience for us.

From there, we took our time driving no more than 200 miles each day and spent time at Graceland in Memphis, Tennessee. It was my fifth trip there and Bob's third. Both being big Elvis Aron Presley fans, we enjoyed stopping at his mansion every chance we got. It is a landmark at which everyone can marvel, regardless of whether or not he/she is an Elvis fan. On that trip we also stopped in Tupelo, Mississippi and saw Elvis' birthplace home, chapel, and museum, something neither of us had done before. The home had been built by Elvis' father, Vernon and Vernon's brother and had only cost them $180. Three years later it was repossessed. Elvis had been asked if there was ever something he wanted in his honor and he had said he'd like a chapel where people could meditate. So in 1979, two years after his death, a chapel was put up on the property where his birthplace was, in his memory. The only trouble was that they did not let us sit and meditate. They had the pews roped off. The museum was built in 1992 and had many items, especially letters, which were not in any of the Memphis museums. We were glad we stopped, as one of the things we learned was that Vernon's brother, Vestus, married Gladys' sister and Vernon's middle name was Elvis. Elvis' middle name Aron was one of Vernon's best friends. His twin brother Jesse Garon was born 35 minutes before Elvis was born and died the following day. Elvis' first public appearance at age 10 was at a Mississippi fair.

We had a glorious time spending part of the autumn season on the Natchez Trace that was the path the Indians took through Mississippi before it became a pony-express route. It had been kept up for travelers to see how it used to be. It went all through wilderness areas and was a beautiful drive. It went from Nashville, Tennessee to Natchez, Mississippi (440 miles), but we only took about 160 miles of it in Mississippi. It was a serene place to celebrate my birthday with a dinner that Bob cooked. We saw many Confederate flags for sale as well as boiled peanuts. We bought the peanuts very hot and tried them out. The man who sold them said it was an acquired taste to get to like them, and we thought he was right.

As we turned into a campground near New Orleans, Louisiana we discovered that the ball of the hitch had broken off and it was only the safety chains that were keeping the car attached. How we found that out was when Bob was making a turn into the campground, he noticed in his mirror that the car wasn't following. The wires that connected the lights were dragging and had ripped apart. It was Saturday night and we felt very fortunate that we were already at the campground. It was no problem getting it fixed the next day. The other lucky thing that happened to us was during our trip to South Carolina when our friend noticed that the brake fluid had completely drained out of the tow car. If he hadn't noticed that, we could have been in big trouble. We got the feeling that God was looking out for us.

We took the car into New Orleans and enjoyed a nice dinner at Felix's on Bourbon and Iberville Streets, a place Bob had frequented when he used to go there on business. After fixing the hitch, we left for Houston, Texas and stayed at the Houston Habitat affiliate like we did in 1998, in their parking lot, plugged into their electric service. We visited with friends from that previous build and with another Habitat friend we had met in Americus. We also drove around the neighborhoods to see the 100 houses we had built in 1998 and they all looked very nice. Since we left in 1998, Anchor fencing had been put around each one of the houses. Often we are asked about how the Habitat homes were taken care of by their owners. HFHI has a follow-up program and we have been pleased at those we have visited years later. The Houston skyline at night had the buildings lighted around most of the square tops. We toured the Houston Astros Enron Field during the day, which was not long after it opened. It had natural grass and a retractable roof in order to have the park air-conditioned in Houston's summer heat. The roof was built of three panels, which could open or close in 20 minutes. There were three levels of green seats. Some of the seats in left field extended into the playing area, giving home-run hitters an advantage. There was a really neat full-sized locomotive that ran on the 800-foot track located above left and center fields. There was a flagpole in dead center field, which was in play. We had been to the Houston Astrodome before the new stadium, then called Enron Field, had been built. There was really no comparison. The new field, besides all its modern features, could also allow fans to watch a game out in the open on days that were not too hot. That was what we loved about baseball, being able to sit outside to watch on a nice day.

We arrived back at Lagoons RV Resort on October 10th to begin the activities we were involved in when we left there five months before. It was good to greet our old friends again and get to know many others, too. When I walked Baggins I found that the pond was almost gone due to the extreme heat and dry spell in Texas that past summer. Even so, there was a rosetta spoonbill. The same two horses were still

grazing around the pond and again were our backyard neighbors during our stay. We also had an opportunity to see armies of ants in the process of carrying leaves to their nesting hills. It was a truly amazing sight to see how far they walked in line formation and how much they could carry. They must be the most industrious inhabitants of our planet.

Many of the men at the campground, like Bob, enjoyed keeping busy and a building project was a terrific way to get them involved in the community. The owner of Lagoons offered to donate supplies and labor for a second Habitat for Humanity house in Rockport. He was a contractor and built the campground himself, with the volunteer help of men like Bob who also took pleasure in construction. He was also involved in building houses in the community and Bob helped him out a little on his own house. The family had been living in the residence behind the office at the campground. They came from Kelowna, British Columbia to settle in Rockport for that venture. It was a beautiful, concrete campground with a huge clubhouse, grassy sites with lots of trees. So Bob was asked to be the house leader for that Habitat project in Rockport, a project he took on with relish. That time he was involved with permits, the foundation, getting other volunteers, providing lunches, picking out and transporting supplies, working with the homeowner to be sure she got her sweat-equity hours, coordinating efforts with the president and treasurer and other board members, planning the dedication ceremony in addition to getting the house built. Bob had to monitor the grant monies for the Lions Club International that were strictly designated to build a handicapped-accessible home. Each year the Lions Club International provided grants to nonprofit-charitable organizations that built or remodeled houses for the physically challenged. All the planning made the fall go by very quickly and before we knew it, we were celebrating New Year's Eve.

*"We can choose whether to be
another brick in the wall or a window."*
— From *A Thousand Paths To A Peaceful Life*
by David Baird

Chapter Six

Our Fourth Year - North to Alaska

Our Journey in 2001

**From Texas through Nevada, Montana to British Columbia through the
Yukon Territory on the Alaskan Highway to Alaska,
across Canada to New York and Maryland, Pennsylvania to Texas**

We started the New Year with our youngest son, Joshua visiting in Rockport, Texas at Lagoons RV Resort for the first 10 days. That year we picked him up at the airport in Houston, Texas so that we could show him around the city of Houston. We took him to meet one of the Habitat owners for whom we had built a house back in June of 1998. Mario was thrilled that we stopped by and he showed Joshua how much he had appreciated our volunteer efforts by giving him all sorts of photographic equipment, after finding out that Joshua was interested in photography. We did a little sightseeing in Houston to show Joshua the man-made waterfalls and the beach at Galveston. We also pointed out the unusual way that Houston showed its street names from sparkling chrome spheres hanging in the middle of the intersections.

Joshua stayed in the park owners' motor home to sleep and spent the rest of the day with us. We didn't really do much special, just enjoyed having him there with us. The weather was not very cooperative although he did get the opportunity to work on Rockport's Habitat house. We had been there since October when Bob was asked to be the house leader for the Habitat for Humanity affiliate in Rockport and began getting ready for the Lagoons men to volunteer to build the second house for the local affiliate. When the Winter Texans arrived they worked on the first house that had been started in May 2000, before it was time to work on the second house, sponsored by the Lions Club International, with labor supplied by Lagoons RV Resort. The Lions Club had several grants available for projects dedicated to construction for the handicapped. They donated $24,000 for a Habitat house as long as the local Habitat affiliate and the local Lions Club each contributed $5,000. That meant a new learning experience for Bob, having to obtain permits, attend meetings, ready the site and pour the concrete. Brian Pahl, the owner of Lagoons, with all his construction experience was a tremendous help. When he wasn't at the site, he was available for answering questions. He knew many of the sub-contractors and suppliers and Habitat benefited by his generous donation of time and expertise. He also encouraged Bob to use his workcamping hours for Habitat. Bob still took care of the campground indoor-heated pool and spa, but instead of all the other work he usually did for the park owner, he worked at the Habitat house. The slab was poured on January 16th and after that Bob worked every day all day, except Sundays so I didn't see much of him. I worked on the house a little and supplied lunches now and then, but mostly I spent afternoons in the clubhouse teaching bridge. I made a lot of new friends that way and enjoyed seeing others learning to take pleasure in bridge.

Meanwhile, we continued to square dance, play bridge with other couples in the evening and attend weekly church dinners and Bible studies. We continued to go to various churches in the area, sometimes there at the campground, but mostly to Coastal Oaks Church. I also volunteered, now and then, at the Humane Society, cleaning cat cages when I wasn't nursing my knee or bronchitis, which I had twice and Bob caught three times during the winter months. In previous years in Rockport the weather had been much kinder. The activities director at Lagoons planned lots of clubhouse activities and we attended a potato bake, ice cream socials, jam sessions, Western Night, a sock hop, and an all-male wedding. Western Night was lots of fun especially because it included a big jail where we paid to have somebody put in jail and then paid to get out again. All that money, about $800, was collected for charity. Lagoons RV Resort participated in many charities, including Habitat and a Mexican ministry. Many people dressed in 50s outfits for the sock hop. It was fun to have music to jitterbug to instead of the usual country music that was everywhere in the South.

We saw the funniest wedding we could have imagined one Sunday evening. It was an all-male cast, including the pregnant bride, bridesmaids, flower girl, and all the guests. Picture those old men going into a thrift store to buy dresses and high heels and then putting on garter belts and stockings, wigs, and fingernail polish. Then they acted their parts for a hillbilly wedding. It was hysterical. Bob was the father of the bride. He wore one boot and one sneaker. The preacher had a peace sign around his neck. One of the men was carrying a shotgun because it was a shotgun wedding. Some of the men I didn't recognize, even after I knew who they were. They wore short skirts, big bosoms, longhaired wigs, make up, you name it! Even the guys who were dressed as men wearing black fingernail polish on their teeth to look like they were missing front teeth were unrecognizable. One of them pretended to be a little boy, with a lollipop and pinwheel. During the ceremony, he yelled, "I have to pee", got up and ran toward the bathroom, then came back with his crotch all wet, like he didn't make it! So many funny things went on.

February 24th was a very busy day for us, and a rewarding one, too. It was the culmination of a lot of hard work on the second Habitat house in Rockport. Most of the men who worked on the house, their wives, and four women in addition to the homeowner and her family attended the Habitat celebration. It was planned with music, singing, speeches, thanks, flowers and everyone seemed to find the dedication very moving. The homeowner was 60 years old, disabled, and lived with her 15-year-old mentally handicapped grandson. She did a lot of work on her own house, working on her required sweat-equity hours. Although the house was ready for her she could not move in until all her hours were completed. We had a lunch in the backyard after the ceremony. We served about 65 people. Bob's usual house leader duties did not include planning the dedication, but that time he was involved in many facets that should have normally been done by the local affiliate, but they seemed to want Bob to take over. It was a great experience for him.

That same evening Lagoons had their annual talent show and once again it was very good. This year, I participated in a Dalmatian dog costume, running between skits down the aisles, shouting "Who let the dogs out - who - who - who?" That song was popular then. During the next two weeks, the weather cooperated as we enjoyed some relaxation time and some beach time on the Gulf of Mexico while we got ready to leave Rockport on March 10, 2001. We drove about four hours from Rockport into Progresso, Mexico for our yearly dental checkups. Going to the dentist in Mexico was very much less expensive than in the States. We had been recommended a particular dentist and although we waited a long time to see him, he was experienced and professional. The girls he had helping him dressed in what we considered to be party dresses. We could sign in at the dentist's office in the late morning and have lunch in a Mexican restaurant while we waited to be seen by the dentist. Tasting authentic Mexican food was a real treat for us. There was always someone employed to sing while walking around the restaurant, which added to the special atmosphere. Sopapillas, a Mexican dessert, made of kneaded flour and shortening, then deep-fried and served in three-inch squares with honey, became a favorite of ours. The streets of Progresso were lined with Mexican wares and vendors sometimes chased us down a street, lowering his prices, to entice us to buy. There were many stores in which to buy medicine and we didn't need a prescription to purchase drugs that had been prescribed. The prices had been cut dramatically.

In Mission, Texas further south in the Rio Grande River Valley, near the Mexican border, we stayed with friends on a site next to the one they owned in a resort just for recreational vehicles. There were many communities in southern regions such as that for people who wanted to own their land but also wanted the option of being able to travel whenever the mood struck. They took us sightseeing to the Los Ebanos Ferry Junction, which was the only operating hand-drawn ferry in the United States. It took us across the Rio Grande River from Sullivan City, Texas to Los Ebanos, Mexico. Back in Texas we saw the famous South Texas green jay, which birdwatchers came from all over the world to observe.

When we left Mission it was not until we got into El Paso, Texas about 800 miles later, that we saw a Wal-mart or anything besides small towns, prairies, and mountains in the distance. That might give the reader an idea about how huge the state of Texas is. Phone booths were only 25 cents. That was a first in a long time! We stayed on Amistad Lake near Del Rio where the water was 39 feet below normal because of drought conditions. We saw lots of prickly pear cacti and aloe vera plants with huge blossoms in that West Texas area. In Big Bend National Park, there were wild flowers everywhere, the best showing in 10 years, lots of bluebonnets (which were actually purple or white) and rocknettles which were yellow. There were many scenic views throughout Big Bend where canyons and mountains are plentiful. It was there that we bought a national park pass. For $50 we could get into all the national parks free for one year. We knew we were going to many national parks in 2001 so our $50 was well spent. It covered both of us. We stayed at a campground outside of Big Bend where Baggins could walk in the riverbed of the Terlingua Creek just behind the campground. It was easy to get to and we could walk for miles, watching what the river had done to the land and how the water had receded badly. Where the water used to run about 50 feet wide, it was running only about three feet wide at that time. We drove through Big Bend National Park on the United States side near Santa Elena, Mexico, walked down a long path to the river, and then took the ferry that was a guy in a rowboat who spoke no English. For two dollars, he took us across in 30 seconds. There wasn't much to see in the town but we wanted to have that experience. Big Bend campgrounds were full because of so many spring breakers. That surprised us.

Texas was one of the states that allowed overnight parking in the rest areas, which was good because there were not many Coast to Coast parks along that part of our travels. We got a little stuck in a gas station because there was no sign about how tall the roof was. It wasn't quite tall enough for the motor home so we had to back out. That meant having to unhook the car. In the first three years of our journey, we only once had to unhook the car because of miscalculations. In those two weeks, we had to unhook the car three times. Besides getting stuck, the gas cost $1.64 per gallon, which at that time was considered very high. The next time we stopped for gas it was $1.25. The ups and downs amazed us. We spent part of a day in El Paso, eating corned beef and cabbage, but not the green beer, at Bennigan's on Saint Patrick's Day. We stayed in state parks in New Mexico and Colorado, which were very picturesque and had lots of room for Baggins to run.

We spent our first Colorado night with snow just north of Colorado Springs. We went to Rocky Mountain National Park in Estes Park, Colorado from there. Due to the snow not all roads were opened in the park. We saw elk near Bear Lake in great scenery. A deer ran across the road, banging right into the driver's side of a car, seemed stunned and kept on going. The tallest peak was Long's Peak at 14,209 feet. We were too early in the season to see the wildflowers that blossomed in June and July, so we didn't see much color but we did view gorgeous snow-covered mountains. It was

too cold and icy for us to think about hiking, however.

Camping at a Bureau of Land Management spot in Carrizozo, New Mexico called Valley of Fires had an exquisite view for us of white sand mountains on either side of the motor home. We enjoyed the wonderfully designed and labeled trail through the lava rock. The lava had run there 3,000 years before, a hot bright orange liquid, two to five miles wide for about 44 miles. When the liquid became cold it formed black and red rocks, still there at the time we were there. The lava rock there was not from a volcano as one might imagine. The earth had opened up when that happened.

What was good about camping out of season in a beautiful area like Trinidad Lake State Park in Colorado, right on a man-made lake, damming the Pergatoire River, surrounded by mountains, was that I could walk Baggins in the closed area and he could have lots of freedom. As we left the town of Trinidad, we noticed that the high school had a gold-domed gym building, the only one we had ever seen, except at the University of Notre Dame.

We stopped on the way to see the Colorado Rockies Coors Field in Denver, Colorado in our quest to visit all the major league baseball parks. That was one of the ballparks that was designed similarly to the one in Baltimore, Maryland combining the nostalgic feel of the 1920s urban stadium with 21st century technology and conveniences, located 21 feet below street level, with the city of Denver and the Rocky Mountains in the background. One of Coors Field's special features was its clock, a meeting place for fans just outside of the park. To mark one mile above sea level was a row of purple seats in the midst of all the other seats that wrapped around the entire upper deck of Coors Field. Behind the right field fence were the bullpens and a tree/rock covered mountain scene that contained water fountains.

Then we visited very interesting friends we had only seen briefly when they visited in New Jersey previously. We had only been in touch through Christmas cards. They already had two grown sons when they adopted four girls, who when we visited, were preteens and teens. They had recently fostered a baby and her two-year-old sister whom they were going to be adopting soon. It was wonderful to visit with such a loving family. Sometimes we missed that. Neither of us was brought up in a large family. I was an only child and Bob had only one sibling.

Having had a problem with the motor home we spent the entire next day in a service station and could only hope that the expensive work they did there would keep us in good stead for our anticipated Alaska trip. However, as we discovered going through so many mountains after that, our temperature buzzer came on any time we went up a hill. In Colorado, there were many hills. It had become very annoying and we didn't know whether or not we actually had an overheating problem since the wires were fixed or perhaps our temperature buzzer was working improperly. We had to put up with that annoyance until we got settled in Pahrump, Nevada in April.

We stayed at a wonderful park on the Ute Indian Reservation in Southwestern Colorado for four days while we toured surrounding states in the car and took a day to

relax and give Baggins a chance to run free for as far as the eye could see, all fenced in with mountains in the background. He was able to chase all the prairie dogs he could find. They always got into their holes before he got to them, though. We visited Mesa Verde National Park in Southwestern Colorado named for Mesa Verde's Spanish green table. It has a unique cultural and physical landscape, reflecting 700 years of history. We could see the cliff dwellings that represented where the Ancestral Pueblo people had lived. They were sheltered in alcoves of the canyon walls. We did not take the time to explore the world-class archeological sites.

We chose not to spend the money for the Four Corners, the only place in the United States where four states (Arizona, Colorado, New Mexico, and Utah) border each other, although we did put our feet on the spot where the states met. We drove through Arches National Park in Moab, Utah where there were over 1,500 arches of various kinds. Arches National Park has the largest concentration of natural stone arches in the world, offering spectacular displays of the natural forces of erosion.

Arches National Park is full of red rocks that had been eroded out from weather conditions to form arches high up above us. It was a beautiful sight. On the way into Canyonlands National Park, we saw rock climbers way up in the steep mountains, appearing like ants from where we were looking. Canyonlands, also in Moab, was filled with mountains and canyons and more strange-rock formations. There was much open range in Utah so cows and sheep just wandered around, sometimes on the roads. We were surprised to see so many oil wells going strong in that part of Utah. Southern Utah turned out to be one of our very favorite places to sightsee.

We left the Ute Indian Reservation and stopped at the Natural Bridge Monument where we could view three different bridges made in the huge rocks from water flowing through the ages. That was where we learned the difference between what they call arches and what they call bridges were formed. They looked the same to us. Bridges are always found in the bottom of canyons where water from streams or rivers had eroded the canyon walls. We saw the second largest bridge of this type in the world. The largest is also in Utah, Rainbow Bridge, but it could not be seen from a car. Arches were formed by the weathering of openings in vertical slabs of sandstone. The alterations could happen because of rain, wind or movements of the earth and took a very long time to form. Opinions varied as to how big an opening must be before it can be classified as an arch, but park officials considered arches to be any opening extending at least three feet in any direction.

Route 95 between Natural Bridges Monument and Capitol Reef National Park in Sorrey, Utah was exquisite. We traveled through red mountains alongside the Dirty Devil River, crossed the Colorado River and crossed a bridge that overlooked the river with steep rocks on either side of us. That river went through Glen Canyon Recreational Area. There was such an array of contrasting colors, deep reds, pink, peach, tan, black, green, and white. We felt at times like we must be in Egypt (not that we had ever been in Egypt, but that was how it felt) with the massive formations of all descriptions on every side of us. Some of the rock looked like huge piles of sand - enormous and expansive.

It was hard finding a campground in March in what seemed like the middle of nowhere at a time when most tourists didn't travel until the weather turned warmer. We passed very few vehicles. It must have been different when the summer tourists came. On our way through Capitol Reef National Park, named for the domed-shaped formations, the road followed the Fremont River. It was always so peaceful for us to drive next to water. The rock formations got even bigger. Even looking from the big motor home windows we couldn't always see to the peaks. It got very cold and very windy in the snow-covered mountains. The buzzer was constant as we went uphill. We were fortunate that the roads were clear, although winding and narrow. Route 12 between Capital Reef National Park and Bryce Canyon National Park was much too steep for us at 14 percent grades. So it was a long haul, going slowly and listening to the buzzer. The canyons on either side of the road were similar to Grand Canyon, with the Escalante River at the bottom. Utah labels its scenic roads "The Scenic Byway". The scenery made these roads definitely worth the trouble.

At Bryce Canyon National Park the wind picked up a lot. There was much snow and many closed trails, so we took the car in to see the exquisite view of the amphitheater, columns of cinnamon-colored rock over a vast area of canyon. As we left Bryce in Bryce Canyon, Utah on Route 12 very near Route 89, we drove under two huge red arches that spread right over our road. Just when we thought we couldn't top the scenery we'd seen on Route 95 and Route 12, we entered Zion National Park in Springdale, Utah. Red-colored rocks had been ground up on top of the asphalt to give the roads a deep red color. The road wound around, many in complete U-shapes, very narrow, very steep, with gorges, canyons, and gigantic high mountains with rock formations all in one place, over and over. It was not something I can describe accurately. Utah is a state that we would definitely recommend. It was absolutely amazing for miles and miles and miles in the southern areas.

We arrived in Las Vegas, Nevada in time for Bob's birthday. With so many choices, he decided that we should go out to dinner and go to a show. We saw *Bottoms Up* in the afternoon, a part girly, part comedy show with impersonations thrown in, quite entertaining. The shows in Las Vegas had a full range of prices from free to hundreds of dollars. We spent four days in Las Vegas, mostly shopping for a recliner and carpeting for the motor home. We were successful and when we got to Pahrump to stay at Preferred RV Park, our Coast to Coast home park, where we had stayed three times before, we put the carpet in and our 1989 Holiday Rambler motor home looked much improved. The carpet was more like the color of Baggins' fur so the floor wouldn't show so much of his hair. He definitely sheds a lot all year round.

While in Pahrump, Nevada we visited friends we'd met there before, played bridge and had our son, John come to visit at Easter time. We took him into Las Vegas where he'd never been before and showed him around. We loved to visit the New York New York Casino because it looked and felt like being in New York City, including all the smells. We saw pirates fighting a battle from their ships at the Treasure Island Casino. We viewed the unbelievable free musical dancing water show outside of the Bellagio's Casino and also viewed that show from the replica of the Eiffel Tower at the top of the Paris Casino which must indeed resemble the famous city of Paris, France. The free gardens inside Bellagio's were exquisite. They changed with the seasons and we had been fortunate to see at least three changes. We went down into the old part of Las Vegas on Freemont Street and took in the free light show that spanned the sidewalk areas. As we walked in and out of casinos, it was fun to put a quarter into the one-armed bandits now and then. The slot machines were more automated than in past visits and some of them didn't even have a handle to pull, but a button to push, instead. On Freemont Street some slot machines took dimes, nickels, and even pennies. Then we took John to some of the great places to eat there in Pahrump. We could eat at the casinos within walking distance of the campground for as cheaply as two dollars per dinner. Breakfasts were even less expensive. Many years ago one could eat cheaply in Las Vegas, too, but not any more. Our friends from Lagoons came to Preferred to stay for two weeks while we all got our vehicles ready for our Alaska trip. The weather turned great and the outdoor-heated pool was fantastic.

NORTH TO ALASKA

We left Pahrump, Nevada on May 5, 2001 with our friends. They had a fifth-wheel trailer pulled by a diesel truck and we had our motor home, towing a car. We traveled through Nevada and found a strange kind of campground hidden behind a casino/bar. The building as well as the town was called Majors Place, which was actually on the map, but consisted of nothing but that building. We were lucky to spot it from the road because there was nothing else around and no signs at the place. The next day after traveling through the Great Basin National Park, the four of us met up with another couple also from Lagoons with whom we had planned our travels. They were in a fifth-wheel trailer with three cats and a dog named Maggie. They had been visiting their family in Provo, Utah. They were Mormons, also known as Latter Day Saints, which gave us a big advantage when we did our sightseeing of Salt Lake City, including Temple Square. We learned that the basic difference between the beliefs of the Latter Day Saints from other Christian denominations was their belief that Jesus appeared in America after His resurrection. Mormons learned of that from the writings of Joseph Smith found in New York, which became the Book of Mormon that they use in addition to the Old and New Testaments of the Bible. We also got to see Brigham Young University and especially liked the underground library. For some reason we didn't realize until later, we missed seeing the Great Salt Lake.

There was a lot of lava rock on both sides of the road near Pocatello, Idaho. We took a side trip in the car to see the Craters of the Moon National Monument near Arco, Idaho which was full of lava rock. Back on the road in our rigs, we ran into a sandstorm that closed Route 15 that we were on. The locals said that it happened often. When the sand blew across the road there was no visibility. Because of the detour, we accidentally got to see Idaho's State Vietnam Memorial in Idaho Falls. In Montana, we crossed the Missouri River several times with beautiful scenery on all sides - mountains, greenery, huge fields - between Helena and Great Falls.

On May 11th we arrived in Lethbridge, Alberta, Canada. There we saw High Bridge, a famous railroad bridge and park. One of the university buildings was set between two hills, unusual architecture as the building was actually connected to the hills on both sides. We saw that again at a Visitors Center when we toured Head-Smashed-In Buffalo Jump at Fort Macleod, Alberta. There were many such jumps to be viewed in Canada and in the northern United States where the Indians used to herd the buffalo over cliffs in order to kill them for food and clothing. We took Route 2 around Calgary and attended a very different Catholic Church in Red Deer,

Alberta. The atmosphere was like that of a Protestant Church with lots of talking, friendly people, a bake sale going on in the hallway, no kneelers, no missals, words for upbeat songs from overhead projectors on the walls, lots of singing, and a sermon about Mother's love, which was a nice start to our Mother's Day, as we were all there together without our children.

We finished our Mother's Day with a Vietnamese dinner at the West Edmonton Mall, the largest mall in the world. It was something! **Under one roof**, it had an amusement park with indoor roller coaster, a water park with a wave pool, bungee jumping, submarine rides, a replica of the Santa Maria, remote control boats in a lake, an ice skating rink, a rooftop driving range, miniature golf, and several recreation rooms in the midst of 800 stores, 110 restaurants and three movie complexes. It had the largest parking area for cars of anywhere else in the world. It was all just gigantic, but we were not in the least bit tempted to bungee jump!

We were finding out more about Canada. We saw a billboard advertising the Loonie Store. That is the United States equivalent of our dollar store. There are no paper bills less than five dollars in Canada. The loonie is a one-dollar coin and the toonie is a two-dollar coin. Most of the showers in Canadian campgrounds were loonie showers, meaning that they were coin operated. That was a surprise for it was the first experience we encountered timed showers that we had to pay for. The owners of our campground in Texas were from British Columbia, Canada, so it was fun hearing that same accent all through Canada, eh? Many products in the grocery stores had the labels in both English and French.

When we got into the Province of British Columbia, Canada, we started on the Alaska Highway, also called the AlCan which had its beginning in Dawson Creek, British Columbia. We traveled on 10 kilometers of the Old Alaska Highway, across the Kiskatinaw Bridge, the oldest wooden trestle bridge in Canada. (When we had been in Kelowna, British Columbia a couple years before, we had taken a hike over an old trestle bridge that had been converted for walkers and bikers.) Every now and then along our way, we would see other parts of the Old Alaska Highway which was at some time rerouted to make the road a little straighter. We also crossed over the Peace River Bridge. We were surprised to find out that the miles weren't marked, even though we had bought the *Mile Post* book, which told about everything along each mile of the road. We synchronized our global positioning with the book's suggested routing by resetting the trip gauge next to our odometer. When we got into Alaska, back in the great USA, we once again enjoyed viewing the mile markers on the roadways which were absent in Canada. The six of us had a great time caravanning along, taking turns leading or following. We each had a CB radio by which to communicate. One of the fellows, a former school principal, loved telling us little stories as we drove along. The lead vehicle would alert the rest of us about severe bumps or wildlife sightings. There were sometimes 30 to 40 degree differences in the daytime and night temperatures. It was in the 60s or 70s and very sunny every day. We had rain only once and that was during the night. The gas was high priced and we certainly had to use a lot of it. Campground prices were also higher than we were used to, but not too bad, taking into consideration the value of the dollar in Canada. It was 55 percent of what the American dollar was worth stateside. We ate food in our rigs to cut costs and often all six of us sat at a picnic table sharing whatever we brought.

It was a long drive across British Columbia as we began winding our way up into the northernmost section of the Rocky Mountains. There were beautiful views of the rugged Rockies. The lower slopes were covered in thick forest while the mountaintops were either bare or covered in a heavy layer of snow. We ran into some snow over the higher passes. We also ran into our first section of unpaved highway under construction. We soon learned that with such a short summer there was always construction going on to fix the roads to and from Alaska, so delays were inevitable and could be expected at any time, every year. From Fort Nelson, we continued to see more farmland, which gradually gave way to forests, much of which had been clear cut and replaced with tree farms. We were reminded that we were in Canada and not in the USA when we went to a local Safeway store where we discovered we had to pay a quarter to use a shopping cart, somewhat akin to baggage cart rentals at airports in the USA. However, the quarter was returned after the user returned the cart and locked it up again.

On the way to Liard River, we had a big day for seeing wildlife. It turned out to be the only day we saw so much wildlife. Among the animals we noted were stone sheep (indigenous to the Stone Mountain Provincial Park area), mule deer, caribou, coyotes, black bears, wild horses. We crossed the Tetsa and Toad rivers and the ice-covered Muncho Lake with its incredibly deep turquoise blue color that sparkled in the sun while resonating a faint tinkling sound like wind chimes as the ice was breaking up under the solar warmth. A great portion of the Trout River was covered with ice and snow and backgrounded with snow-covered mountains. Just before reaching the Trout River, we saw a big black bear. The environ's panoramic beauty and highly abundant wildlife display made this part of the trip a magnificent experience!

The road was very winding. When we got to British Columbia's Liard Hot Springs, we found a well-kept boardwalk in the provincial park leading to the natural hot springs located in the woods, with a bathhouse for changing. With the outside 40 degree temperatures, we were glad not having to wear wet bathing suits on the long boardwalk back to our campsite. Not only were the hot springs wonderfully exhiliarating and conveniently accessible to the provincial park's campground, but it was all free. Dave and Mary Lazor had told us about Liard Hot Springs. Their trip tip was truly worth the miles traveled! The natural setting where the hot springs were located visually added to the ambiance of the park. Due to its unique design, visitors can choose a pool water temperature suited to their personal like: hot, hotter or hottest. Water flowing nearest from the spring's upper source is most warm. Configured in several levels, there are multiple ponds where the water becomes cooler at each descending level. As the waters course in a waterfall spillover manner from one level to the next, the spring's bather can indulge in a refreshing splashdown by the mineral-rich heated waters flowing from the upper to the lower pools. We could have sat for hours savoring the area's scenery. Visible across the road of the provincial park's campground was a grazing buffalo. I was walking Baggins when we came up to the buffalo and realizing it was real and not a lifelike re-creation, we backed up slowly. Among other wildlife, we saw wild horses roaming in that area.

From there, we crossed a bridge over the Coal River into the Yukon Territory. Those roads got really bumpy. All sorts of stones accumulated in the car's windshield wiper well and where the tow bar was hitched. When we got into Watson Lake, Yukon, a town of about 17,000 residents, our vehicles were covered in mud. A usual experience for people arriving in Watson Lake, the campground had nine spaces set aside with hoses and brushes so that we could have washed our rigs, but we didn't. It was too cold. Watson Lake's main claim to fame was its world famous signpost forest. A homesick soldier working on the Alaska Highway in 1942 wanted to inscribe his hometown name and the mileage to Watson Lake by placing the first sign during World War II. Since, people had hung over 40,000 signs identifying them and their hometowns. There were signs left by people from all over the world and they were made from all kinds of materials. Some people had left their vehicle license plates. Some had plaques made professionally. Many were homemade, spur-of-the-moment plaques. The signs went on and on for blocks. Across from the campground was a two-mile trail around Nye Lake. Bob, Baggins, and I took a very scenic walk that day. The Visitors Center had a good slide show about Alaska's part in building roads during World War II.

We were in the Yukon Territory at Mile Post 698 when we crossed the Continental Divide, passing great scenery with more snow-covered mountains, many rivers, and trees uncountable. Wherever the road twisted, the tall mountains were in front of us with breathtaking views of the Cassiar Mountains. Beside us were many small creeks and ponds. We crossed the Nisutlin Bay Bridge, the longest bridge on the Alaska Highway, just before Teslin. In itself, the highway was an amazing feat when you think about the short time in which that road was built. Americans were in a hurry to get their country protected and completed the highway in about nine months.

Arriving at Yukon's capital and largest city, Whitehorse is located on the Yukon River and boasts a population of 30,000 residents. We drove to a suspension bridge and walked a trail which followed the river for a couple of miles before looping back through a forest. It was a lovely hour walk with birch trees starting to leaf out and a few hardy wildflowers blooming in the sunny areas along the trail. From our stance, we were able to look down at the vibrant green waters and looking up to see the skyward-directed trees and the steadfast mountains. We walked to the remains of Canyon City, what used to be an old settlement within the woods and then walked back on the trail that used to carry trams that hauled supplies to the settlement. There were many unleashed pet dogs running free on that path. Mountain bikers also seemed to enjoy the trail. What a stunning climb! One thing we had trouble adapting to as we went further north was the continuous daylight. In Whitehorse it didn't even start to get dark until after midnight and then it didn't get real dark and was broad daylight again at three o'clock in the morning. We found ourselves going to bed later and later. In Whitehorse was the Yukon Beringia Interpretive Center, which provided a fascinating look at what scientists had learned about the land bridge that formed between Siberia and North America during the last ice age.

In the Yukon, the Alaska Highway turned from Route 97 to Route 1, which took us to the Kluane Mountain Range and the Kluane National Park where we hiked the Rock Glacier Trail with Baggins. It was very steep, and we could see Saint Elias Lake and Saint Elias Mountain from the top. We passed ice fields, which we learned were at the tops of glaciers. Kluane Lake is the largest natural lake in Canada at 154 square miles and was supposed to be great for fishing but at that time was covered with ice and snow.

Like it's name, the town of Destruction Bay didn't have much to offer, just a gas station and a store. That was rather typical of the towns we passed through on the Alaska Highway. We saw many trees with very big knots in the wood and found out that sometimes the spruce trees were damaged so the tree sent extra sap to the damaged area that caused a huge bulge to grow on the trunk. Those were often used to make furniture. We saw varied shapes and were intrigued.

Baggins and Maggie continued to get along well. Baggins had become quite brave. When we stopped at a rest area he would run outside and sometimes we'd have to start the engine to get him out of the woods when we were ready to leave. He seemed to enjoy himself as much as we did. The roads were a mess partly because of the spring thaw and the permafrost problems. The permafrost stayed all year long below the surface of the ground. When the road heated up, the permafrost at the top thawed enough that it affected the road and caused heaving and big potholes. It got worse farther north. Because of that, by the end of winter the telephone poles were falling over and many were broken. It didn't appear that they had begun their spring repairs yet. Apparently they just didn't have enough time during the summer to get all the pole and road repairs finished. Then the next year, what had been fixed was damaged again. So, it remained an endless battle of nature that caused road delays all year long. When we had gotten reports from other people who had already taken the Alaska Highway, they varied about the state of the roads depending on which year they had gone and how much damage there had been in a particular year. The other causes of delay were construction that would be different also from year to year. So there was really no way to tell ahead of time how good or bad the roads would be. We found them very bumpy and in part almost unmanageable and on some days had to travel quite slowly.

Crossing back into the United States on May 23rd took only a couple of minutes. There was a boundary line cutting through the trees for as far as we could see on both sides of the road. They must have kept it cut for the purpose of showing off the border. We stopped at Border City, just over the United States line into Alaska and found out that others who had not stopped had to turn back because of snow in Tok, the next Alaskan town. We had cold and heavy rains but missed the snow. There the Alaska Highway turned into Route 2. We passed the Tanana River and stopped at Tok, a town of about 1,400, after pulling off to help a van get back on the road when it slid off the shoulder. With that kind of road, it was easy to fall off. They had wanted to pull off to get a picture and the top-heavy van, holding eight students from all over the world, with lots of luggage, just began sliding. We were able to stop a vehicle that had equipment that could pull the van out. While we passed through Tok we learned that one in three Tok residents was involved in some way with sled dogs, giving it recognition as the sled dog capital of the world.

After passing through so many little, little towns, we were happy to get some real groceries at Delta Junction. We still couldn't find many of the foods we usually bought in the lower 48 states. We passed through the town of North Pole. There was nothing much there except a small Christmas store on one side of the road and a big sign on the other side where we stopped to take Christmas pictures. Bob and I were prepared with Christmas vests. We had been amazed and just couldn't get used to the 24 hours of daylight. It just wasn't what we were accustomed to and seemed so strange to be walking the dog at 11 P.M. and still seeing daylight. It seemed no matter when we awakened in the middle of the night, it was still light outside. And yet, it was cold. We spent ten days and about 1,400 miles on the Alaska Highway before getting to Fairbanks, Alaska. There was a dispute whether the Alaska Highway actually ended in Fairbanks or in Delta Junction, 130 miles closer. Apparently  when the army was putting in the highway in 1942 for the war effort, they constructed it until Delta Junction where there was already a road to Fairbanks, but the government took over maintaining that part of the road, so they still considered it the Alaska Highway. We took pictures at both places just to be sure we had the end of the highway.

Once we arrived in Fairbanks where we spent a week, the daytime temperatures were mostly in the 50s and the sky was overcast. When the sun was out, it felt a lot warmer than the temperature said. During the nights, it was still in the 30s so we couldn't dry camp. We needed electricity to keep warm. It would have been cheaper not to have to pay for campgrounds, so planning to be there a little later in the summer might have been a better idea, although the way we did it, we missed many of the tourists. It was also possible that had we traveled later in the season, that we might not have been able to find appropriate spots in which to dry camp. We also were fortunate to miss many of the mosquitoes. There were so many options to weigh when making plans.

Here's a true story for you, one I probably wouldn't have believed had I not been there. On the Saturday before Memorial Day, we mailed a couple of packages and two birthday cards at the local post office in Two Rivers, 27 miles from Fairbanks. We had been told that our mail would not go out until Tuesday because of the holiday, which was no problem for us. However, Memorial Day morning, the post office burned to the ground. That was a sad situation because a young couple owned it along with a grocery store, restaurant and greenhouses under one roof. Everything went to the ground. We had our packages and letters burned right along with it, just a minor inconvenience and expense for us, compared to the hardship of the owners. We certainly had never had anything like that happen before, a really good excuse for not getting a birthday card out in time! The very next morning, the post office was up and running again. Apparently, there was a contingency in place that made a portable station available immediately. Before we left that campground a week later, a space had been rented across the street from the old post office and it was business as usual. What a country!

In Fairbanks, we attended a free theme park called Alaskaland, a collection of historic cabins that had been turned into gift shops, restaurants, and places to dig for gold, which we thought seemed to be run down. They served an Alaskan Salmon Bake but it was expensive so we passed on that. The park also included an air museum that Bob enjoyed. At the University of Alaska, we went to a wonderful museum about Alaska but it was not possible to see the wildlife the University usually had to offer because of problems with hoof and mouth disease at that time.

The six of us took a riverboat cruise aboard the Discovery sternwheeler on the Chena and Tanana Rivers. We were introduced to Susan Butcher, who during four years in the 1980s, was the Iditarod Sled Dog Race winner. The race was 1,200 miles from Anchorage to Nome that took about 15 days through treacherous territory. Susan also had taken a team of dogs up Mount McKinley, an amazing act of skill. We got to see an exhibition from sled dogs trained by an Iditarod rookie and learned that most, but not all sled dogs were Alaskan huskies, a mixed breed. We also watched a native woman fillet a huge salmon and learned all about commercial catching of salmon. We were next taken to an Indian village where we saw reindeer (which were actually just domesticated caribou) with such big antlers. There were all kinds of animal hides. We were instructed about the tanning process and were shown Indian beadwork and a parka that was like the one that Native Indians had on display at the Smithsonian Institute in Washington, DC. We were given fishing techniques at an Athabascan fish camp.

The most exciting part of our Fairbanks stay was getting across the Arctic Circle. That we did in a Cessna 207, a little bush plane. We landed 150 air miles north of Fairbanks, which would have been over 300 road miles, at Bettles, Alaska, at the foot of the Gates of the Arctic National Park. The only way into that park was by plane. They were trying to keep it and Kobuk Valley National Park totally in the wilderness. Only about 1,000 people hike inside those parks each year. Bettles is 33 miles north of the Arctic Circle in the foothills of the Brooks Range. On the plane ride we could see the Yukon River where a bridge was put over it for the pipeline to pass, and we saw many, many miles of the Alaska pipeline. What an extraordinary feat that was to build in the mid-1970s. They put in 800 miles of 48-inch pipe, with 12 pumping stations in less than four years. It crossed three mountain ranges and 70 rivers or streams. Much of the Alaska pipeline was built above the ground because of permafrost. Cooling elements hold up the pipes and also cool the ground so that the oil running inside the pipes won't cause thawing of the ground, which could collapse the structure. The pipeline runs north and south the entire expanse of Alaska. When back on ground, we got to see parts of the pipeline close up.

Just before we left Fairbanks we went to a Gold Rush Camp in Fox, Alaska near our campground in Two Rivers. We enjoyed it a lot because Bob panned for gold while the rest of us watched, lowering the cost, and we got individual attention from the owner because it was early in the tourist season. In the places that sold time to pan for gold, we got to keep very minute pieces that we found. Everybody found some. I had my little pieces put inside a pendant for a necklace. We also went into the center of Fairbanks for our last chance to see the huge Eskimo statue at the Visitors Center and the **End-of-the-Alaska Highway** marker. There were end markers both in Fairbanks and in Delta Junction that declared the end of the highway, a controversial issue that I mentioned before.

It was tough to leave our campsite in Two Rivers because the six of us had been the only ones there with so many trails through the wooded areas in which to walk for miles and miles. That was also the place where one couple parted company with us in order to get home sooner than the rest of us. We wanted our only trip to Alaska to last. That was the beauty of full-time RVing and having few deadlines. On our way to our next stop, we took Route 3, George Parks Highway, and drove on the Alaskan Native Veterans Honor Bridge in Nenana across the Tanana River. Driving beside the Nenana River, we took in the fantastic scenery in this remote corner of the world. A train ran just above the river.

Inside Denali National Park is Mount McKinley, the highest mountain in North America. If its rise is used as the determining factor, it is the tallest mountain in the world, not Mount Everest. But Everest lifts higher into the sky than McKinley. Confusing at first was that the Athabaskan Indians referred to Mount McKinley as the Great One, or Denali. So the national park was eventually renamed from its former identity as Mount McKinley National Park. There are 6 million acres of wilderness in Denali National Park. It is vast and one of the few places left for wild animals to roam. Getting to Denali early in the season meant we had our choice of campgrounds inside the park. Dry camping (having no hook-ups), we experienced a couple of very cold nights without heat. We could walk or take shuttles almost anywhere we wanted to go. I walked both our doggie and our friends' along Riley Creek and we enjoyed that very much. We splashed our feet in the water among the rocks. Our campsites were just perfect for building a fire and roasting marshmallows. For the few hours that we were allowed to run our generator during the day, we hooked up a cord so that our friends would have power, too. Very often, fifth-wheel trailers don't have a generator like our motor home.

Some of the longer shuttle rides had not opened because there was still snow in the higher mountain roads, so we took a six-hour-round-trip shuttle to Eielson Visitors Center instead of the longer trip that would probably have been allowed the following week. We had a driver who was very knowledgeable about the park and stopped whenever any of us pointed out wildlife, so that we could get lots of pictures. We were able to see a silver wolf, which is unusual, as only about 10 percent of the visitors to Denali get to see a wolf. We saw many caribou, three grizzly bears, arctic ground squirrels, ptarmigans which were Alaska's state birds, several sheep and lambs, a few very close to the bus, and a golden eagle. Missing in our tour were moose. Every day we were told by others how close they'd seen a moose, but we did not. We learned that dall sheep were white and had a lighter build and little curl in their horns.

Of course, the reason most people come to Denali is to get a clear view of Mount McKinley. Because it is so high at 23,320 feet, it makes its own weather and clouds usually obstruct it. About 30 percent of people who  visit got to see it clearly, and we did in several different places on our bus trip. It was definitely huge and beautiful, covered in snow, trying to hide behind another array of picturesque mountains, making it obvious how big Denali is. In 1998, during the four summer months that year, Denali was seen clearly on four days only, so we felt really fortunate in 2001.

We learned something about the Alaska landscape on our tour that included wondrous views of the mountains and glacial carved valleys. The vegetation called taiga or boreal forest is the swampy, coniferous forest at the lower levels. It exists as a nearly continual belt of evergreens, many bearing cones as do pine trees. The only evergreens that can survive in the permafrost areas are black spruces that are 150 years old by the time they reach 12 feet tall and three inches in diameter. They just can't get bigger in such cold weather with so much darkness all winter. Although conifers dominate the boreal forest, northern hardwoods that lose their leaves, also called deciduous trees as birch, aspen, and poplar, have established themselves in the more open areas. Vast regions of Canada's boreal or taiga forest were under leases to forestry companies and mostly for the production of pulp and paper. The Alaska boreal forest was mostly being protected for the long-term conservation of healthy-functioning ecosystems, wilderness and wild animals. Considering the other alternative options which our nation's leaders could have taken and we currently see being experienced in the mutilation of the African rain forests for exploitive reasons, we find the preservation of this Alaskan habitat another reason to love America.

The name given to the next level of vegetation is tundra. It is a windswept, cold, barren, treeless area that extends from the tree line to the highest mountain peaks of the northern arctic regions. We started our tour in the taiga forest, but it quickly changed to vast areas of tundra as we climbed up into the Alaska Range. The tops of the higher peaks were bare of vegetation, marked with exposed rock in shades of yellow and orange. The Alaska Range extends throughout South Central Alaska, separating the coastal regions from the tundra prairies of the interior. Mount McKinley is the dominant mountain in the Alaska Range.

In one area of the bus tour we saw the narrow dirt road hug the mountain and on the other side was a shear drop to a beautiful valley and a glacial river far below. The indescribable mountains and the carpet-like skirting of the dark green muskeg surrounding the base points of these enormous multilithic structures makes the visitor feel inferior in comparison to God's craftmanship of these masterpieces.   Muskeg or marsh is also called peat bog and covers more than 10 percent of Southeast Alaska like a soggy blanket draped over the landscape. It is full of green shrubby plants with the ground covered in mosses and grasses. The whole muskeg area is very swampy with numerous ponds and lakes, many with nesting ducks and swans. It is a usually low-lying area of soft waterlogged ground, a soil type, also called wetlands, that is common in the arctic areas.

During our five days in Denali National Park, we took a 2-1/2-mile hike, a rise of 400 feet, traversing up and down hills and taking over an hour. So when we took another hike of about 2-1/3 miles, we thought it would take about the same time. We hadn't read enough or asked enough questions. If we had hiked to the top of Mount Healy, we would have been able to see Mount McKinley, but we didn't get that far. We met other hikers on the trail, some following us up, some coming down and who had not reached the top. The last part of the trail had not yet been zigzagged, so it was super steep with a rise of 1,700 feet. If we had found out more about the trail before we left, we might have realized that we should have spent a whole day with lots of food and more water than we had and taking 20-minute rests on the way. But, we thought it would be like the prior day's hike. It's amazing how the difference between the 400-foot elevation was in comparison to the 1,700-foot rise! Mount Healy Overlook Trail featured several places that overlooked the entire Denali area including the Visitors Center and Denali Hotel. It was nice knowing we were ahead of most of the other hikers since the trails had already started getting crowded. We met on the trail a girl who came from Austria and another from Denmark, both with traveling groups of young people from all over the world. The only animal we ran into on that trail was a huge hare, gray with white trim. He didn't sit long enough to have his picture taken!

We talked with several shuttle-bus drivers and other helpers who came from all over the United States to work there. One lady traveled from Maine to just have something different to do that summer. Everyone we met who worked there was very friendly.

In Denali, visitors were treated to a wonderful free sled-dog demonstration put on by the rangers at the kennel where the dogs were kept during the summer months. During the winter months the dogs were working which is what they loved to do. Because Denali National Park was almost entirely a wilderness area, motorized vehicles were allowed only on the road corridor. The rangers used these dogs in the winter to patrol the park. The Alaskan husky, or just plain husky, is a catchall term for any of the arctic breeds of northern-type dogs, usually cross or mixed-breeds. Their thick coats were just so beautiful.

One evening there was a little outdoor amphitheater at Riley Campground where a ranger gave us a talk on grizzly bears: reasonable and unreasonable fears. She told us that grizzly bears are brown and vary considerably in size depending on the area they inhabited. She said if you saw a grizzly bear not to panic by running, but to look away and wave your arms about as you were slowly backing up. If the bear did approach you, then you should play dead. It was when the bear began to maul you that you then wanted to fight back hard. In most cases, the bear wouldn't want you. It still sounded pretty ominous to us.

When we left Denali National Park, we drove to Talkeetna, which is on the south side of Mount McKinley. There was a ranger station from where the climbers left to head up the mountain. We actually ran into several climbers just getting back. It was the Talkeetna Airport that was the staging area for everybody who climbed Mount McKinley. The climbers and all their gear were flown to a glacier at 7,000 feet from where they began their climb. Everyone had to be off the mountain by early July because after that, there was not enough snow cover on the glacier for planes to safely land. We camped free in the parking lot of the Visitors Center at Talkeetna Junction since it had warmed up enough during the nights to sleep without heat. After paying $12 in the past to dry camp (also called boon docking), we thought free sounded more reasonable. The next night on the way to Anchorage, we also found a place to pull over to dry camp. At that point, we were able to see Mount McKinley clearly again from the road as well as another mountain, called Peter's Dome, which briefly peeked out from behind the clouds. We drove through Wasilla, the home of the Iditarod sled dog race and found more information about that famous yearly race. Trying to fathom the endurance both people and dogs must have had to endure the 1,200 miles they covered from south to north Alaska in 15 days or so and in such a hostilely frigid environment is beyond belief! Many people dedicate their lives to work with and train the dogs for the Iditarod race.

We got to Anchorage and enjoyed the stay in the driveway where Bob's niece lived. Our friends harbored at campgrounds in Anchorage, maintaining contact with us and together continued our area sightseeing. It was fun going to softball games in the evenings. We still couldn't get used to being able to start a ball game at nine o'clock at night. We went to a really neat movie theatre, called Bear Tooth. For a two-dollar admission fee, they seated us at tables, serving us dinner while we watched the movie. We also ate at a bagel restaurant having the ambiance of a hotel lobby, quite different than anything we'd experienced before. We saw the world's largest chocolate fountain in the Alaska Wild Berry Products store and scheduled stops at the Museum of History and Art, Botanical Gardens, Anchorage Fish And Game Headquarters, and played bridge at the spacious Anchorage Senior Center. It was the nicest one we had seen on our journey and they served delicious lunches to anyone who wanted to pay a reasonable price. There were no discounted prices for senior citizens, just generally good food and good prices. While parked in the driveway, we basked in the backyard's sunshine as well as at a nearby park. Almost everywhere the eye could scan in Anchorage was a backdrop of beautiful mountains. One morning while Baggins and I were walking in the park, I thought I was seeing two large brown dogs. They turned out to be twin calves with their mother moose cow right along side of them. It was rare for a moose to have more than one calf and by the time the calf reached 400 pounds the cow put her out on its own and began the process of becoming pregnant for another eight months. We watched for about 20 minutes before they moved on. How exciting for us, but I think the resident Alaskans view moose as we viewed the sight of deer on the East Coast as a fairly mundane experience. We were still enamored by the moose so close by. At home, we loved to see deer near the road, but we didn't stop to take pictures of them like we did with the moose on our journey.

In the middle of our Anchorage stay, the four of us decided to go to the Kenai Peninsula fearing that we may not have been able to reserve a campground in July. So we left Anchorage for a while to go down to Soldotna on the Kenai Peninsula. In order to get there, we drove on Seward Highway through Chugach State Park which borders Anchorage and provides residents with access to their own wilderness. The 6 million acre Chugach National Forest is just east of Chugach State Park and is the second largest national forest in the nation. Tongass National Forest, also in Alaska, is the largest with 17 million acres. That Coast to Coast campground in Soldotna was right on the Kenai River. It was in our system, so we could stay there for a week at five dollars per night. Bob thought he'd do some fishing, but by the time we figured out all the regulations, he thought he'd be safer not to. We did watch lots of other fishermen, though, and got to see lots of big salmon, halibut, and trout being caught. On the way to a spot along the Russian River, it was so crowded that we couldn't get a parking space to watch the fishing. That kind of fishing was called combat fishing because the men and women were all lined up a couple feet apart, each fighting for a space in the water, all hoping to snag that next fish. They were not allowed to use bait for King Salmon, but instead

just tried to get the hook into the fish's mouth. So the fish weren't actually biting; the fisherman kept casting over and over hoping to hook the fish, kind of by accident. That seemed like a really strange way to fish, but there were so many fishermen doing it that it must have been fun for them. The salmon do not eat when they spawn, which is why they have to hook them.

By the time a week had passed, the weather had been so warm that the snow from the mountains caused high waters in the rivers and fishing was no longer very good, as the fish had been driven down into deeper water. The ferry that brought many of the fishermen to the area had to stop running because of high waters. Meanwhile, a big fire had gotten out of control and most of the week we saw and smelled smoke. Many people were watering down their homes just in case the fire spread more. We wanted to stop for buffalo burgers, but restaurants were forced to shut down their propane tanks and close until the threat of fire was over. Fortunately, we could try a buffalo burger when we got back to Anchorage at the Senior Center.

We drove to the southern end of the Kenai Peninsula to Homer Spit, a five-mile bar of gravel that juts out from the Homer shoreline where we saw the fish actually jumping out of the water. We were disappointed to find that area so commercialized, with so many little shops, when we had expected a more natural setting. They had a cute saying in Homer: "Homer - just for the halibut!!" It is the halibut fishing capital of the world. We drove up and down the Cook Inlet and noticed the change in the waters in about four hours time. In the earlier hour we saw lots of the beach (the quicksand type) and by the time four hours had passed, the water was right up to the wooded area with no beach showing. We watched that phenomenon from a steep cliff. Alaska has the second highest tide waters, meaning that within a year's time the waters changed the most from their low point to their high point. (Nova Scotia was the first.) We saw several bald eagles along the way, as Alaska was one of their favorite habitats. We went into Kenai City several times. We saw cranes, caribou, and our first time for seeing a herd of 60 caribou. We had heard about dip netting and thought it would be fun to watch but when we got out to the beach dunes, there was no dip netting at that time. We went to Clam Gulch but picked the wrong time for catching the clams. It should have been done about an hour before the high tide came in. It turned out that it was a good thing we couldn't dig for clams because we learned later that we needed a license even to do that. But we did see a beautiful sunset there at about midnight. Even after the sun set there, it was still light outside. By the way, we've been told that there are no snakes, skunks, or turtles in Alaska and we didn't see any. It must be too cold a climate for them.

When I finished reading the Bible, after eleven months of reading a few chapters at a time, I was sitting at the edge of the Kenai River in such a serene setting. Bob was busy finding out about a Habitat project in Kenai. When we went to see the Habitat house, we also saw a moose cow and calf in the neighborhood. They seemed to stop and pose for pictures for us. The next day Bob returned to actually work on the Habitat house. The other volunteers were from various parts of the country. A church group had brought some of their youth members with them.

We spent some time at the Kenai National Wildlife Refuge which covers almost two million acres within walking distance of our campground. It was hard getting used to Alaska's vastness. There were films being shown at the Wildlife Refuge and we learned a lot about salmon and how they lived for four years from the time they were born in a river, did limitless travel and then ended up in that same river to lay eggs and die. It was an amazing adventure as they traveled against the current. We also viewed Arctic wildlife, including polar bears eating seals and the largest arctic animal, the bowhead whale, eating the smallest life in the sea, strange and wondrous. On the "Keen Eye" (get it? For Kenai) trail, we saw three Alaskan ecosystems: spruce forest with knobby trees, wetlands, and a lake. Part of the trail was on a boardwalk, which has become common to protect wetland areas. One morning when I was taking Baggins for a walk on the road to the Wildlife Refuge, we encountered a moose cow and her calf leisurely crossing our road. Baggins barked and barked, but fortunately the moose must not have seen him as a threat to her calf and they continued on to the other side into the wooded area. The Kenai area was definitely our opportunity to see lots of moose.

After we left the campground, we spent our first night at Quartz Creek State Park, near Cooper Landing on the Sterling Highway, a wonderful place to stay. Baggins and Maggie both enjoyed being so near the water. Then we spent a few nights dry camping in turnouts on the road. That was to make up for all the expensive campgrounds we stayed in on the way to Alaska. It was warm enough so that we could dry camp most of the time. Driving the car to the Russian River Campground, we had heard it was a good spot to see more wildlife. We went on a two-mile hiking trip to see waterfalls within the campground. While there, we saw a black bear and photographed him climbing a tree. A bit further down the road, we saw the biggest male moose we'd seen so far. He crossed the road right in front of us. Of course, we stopped the car to see him.

We took turns watching each other's dog when we took an all-day-boat tour from Seward to Kenai Fjords National Park proving to be an advantage of traveling with another couple. Our boat trip started at Resurrection Bay into the Gulf of Alaska enroute to the Holgate Glacier. That was the most interesting part of the tour. A glacier begins when more snow falls in the winter than melts in the summer. Over tens of thousands of years, that snow builds up and recrystallizes into a solid mass of ice. When the accumulation of ice becomes so great that the force of gravity causes it to move, a glacier is born. There are four types of glaciers and the one we saw was a fjord glacier. That one was calving, producing sounds like a cannon as well as losing pieces in ice falls. Others said that as the ice shifted, it made a sound like rifle shots and the crackling of thunder. It stood huge at 750 feet high, part of the Harding Ice Field. Ice fields span 28,800 of Alaska's 586,412 square miles, about five percent of the land. Harding Ice Field has some 34 glaciers that flow from a 700-square-mile ice pack. The top of the mountain got about 1,000 inches of snow annually. The glacier moved forward toward the water two feet each day. It showed huge cracks and was an incredible sight, a white and blue wall of ice.

After eating a great salmon and chicken buffet lunch, we stopped for about 20 minutes, 300 feet away from the face of the glacier. The islands we passed were teaming with sea lions swimming in the surf and laying around on the rocks at the bottom of the cliffs. Above them were hundreds of nesting tufted puffins. Those comical looking birds had stocky bodies and massive orange and red bills. On another island, the cliffs were covered with thousands of nesting common murres, the Northern Hemisphere's version of the penguin. They looked a lot like penguins but flew well enough to get to their cliff nesting sites. However, like the puffins they were much more at home on the ocean where they fed by diving and flying underwater after small fish. On the return trip we saw several beluga whales, dall porpoises, seals, sea otters and bald eagles.

One of our trips to Seward took us to the beach where there was a wonderful path for dog walking or biking all along the beach from the town to the city parking lot where many campers were dry camping. Our trips to Seward were such beautiful drives. The Seward Highway along the Cook Inlet had some of the prettiest scenery we had seen in Alaska. The road wound around Turnagain Arm (an ocean inlet that had 35-foot-daily tides), then through forested snow-capped mountains. Seward was located in a gorgeous

setting on Resurrection Bay surrounded by mountains. The city had a 300-site campground along the shore of the bay although we chose to dry camp near Glennallen. We left the motor home on the road and took the car to Begich, Boggs Visitors Center near Portage

Glacier. With exhibits, films and attractive surroundings, it was absolutely worth stopping there and we learned some very interesting facts about Alaska.

It is nearly 600,000 square miles, one-fifth the size of the combined lower 48 states with only 15,000 miles of road. It boasts the city furthest north in the United States, Barrows. It has the tallest mountain in North America, Mount McKinley. Lake Hood, in Anchorage near the airport, is the world's largest seaplane base. (We had seen lots of seaplanes, even one in the front yard in a nearby neighborhood.)

That was one of the most informative Visitors Centers we had seen in the United States as well as being in a great setting. There were tremendous pieces of ice in the water in front of the building from the nearby glacier. About 20 years ago the Portage Glacier was right outside the Visitors Center, but had receded so far that it had disappeared around a mountain and left a large lake in its wake. From Seward Highway to Portage Glacier was an awesome drive. The wildflowers had burst into bloom, covering the roadsides and mountain meadows in a riot of color. Then we drove through the longest vehicle tunnel in North America, 2-1/2 miles long from Portage Glacier to Whittier. We had a long wait because it was only one way and the trains and cars from each direction took turns. Turning that railroad tunnel into a car tunnel as well was engineering ingenuity accomplished just two years before. Because we didn't fish, there was nothing special for us to go into Whittier for except to see Prince William Sound and to go through the tunnel. The first year it was opened to cars, the tunnel was free, but that year it cost $15 round trip. It was an experience to see a rough tunnel in comparison to tunnels we had been used to with concrete supports.

We learned even more about Anchorage on our return visit there. It reminded me of Davis, California with all the bike trails. One could bike practically anywhere around Anchorage, around Cook Inlet, as well as beside busy roads because of the way the trails and overpasses were set up. We had two superb days for riding bikes, not too hot, not too cold. It was the first time we had taken our bikes off the back of the motor home since February. Believe me, they were dusty even with a cover. We biked all around the Tony Knowles Coastal Trail, 11 miles each way. It ran right into Earthquake Park Trail, named for the 1964 earthquake that devastated the area. Anchorage had 120 miles of paved biking and walking trails, 87 miles of unpaved trails and many, many local parks. The Balto Seppala Park, where I walked Baggins every morning, was just around the corner from Milky Way Drive near Turnagain Road (How do you like those names?) and seemed to get a lot of use, especially from dog owners. We drove to a very scenic view of Woronzof Point and then also saw it at a distance on one of our bike rides.

Anchorage had a post office near the airport that was open seven days a week, 24 hours a day, and every time we were there it was crowded. At the airport were many, many planes for Federal Express and many, many tugs (the containers that fit neatly inside the Fed Ex planes). We found an unusual type of parking in the neighborhoods. Many houses were built around cul-de-sacs where the lots were all pie shaped with the smallest part in front. There was not room for a car in front of the house so when the driveway was full the cars parked right in the middle of the cul-de-sacs. It still left room for cars to get around the cul-de-sac and it was a convenient place for a family to have an extra car parked.

Many of the stores in Alaska had the word cache in their names: gold cache, hamburger cache, jewelry cache, bridal cache, for example. There was a store called Pull Tabs, which we learned was a place where Alaskans could gamble. When we first saw the sign, we thought it was some kind of recycling center. We visited the Alaska Native Medical Hospital that had been recommended to us because of the Alaskan artwork in all the hallways. It was a new facility, built for Native Alaskans, Indians and Eskimos. Another way we had found during our travels to find good, inexpensive meals was to frequent hospital cafeterias. Near the hospital was the University of Alaska at Anchorage which everybody called UAA. That was a very nice campus. Even though Bob's niece had a teaching degree from Colorado University at Boulder, it took her two years on a waiting list to get into the teaching system in Alaska. We attended the Vineyard Church, which was unusual because the congregation sat around tables so they could bring in coffee and other drinks while participating in the service.

We found many signs in Alaska that differed from those in most of the lower 48 states. Some examples were: DON'T TRASH ALASKA; DRIVE WITH HEADLIGHTS ON AT ALL TIMES; DOG TEAM CROSSING; AVALANCHE AREA NEXT 1.5 MILES; GIVE MOOSE A BRAKE; FIRE DANGER VERY HIGH TODAY; DELAY OF 5 VEHICLES ILLEGAL / MUST USE TURNOUTS; IN CASE OF EARTHQUAKE, GO TO HIGH GROUND OR INLAND.

Wildflowers were abundant in Alaska. They made the sides of the roads look nice. It seemed that some people didn't always mow their lawns as frequently as others because they would have to mow down the pretty wildflowers. Some residents dug up the ones in the lawn and transplanted them to a common area. Others dug them up from wilder areas to transplant them to their yards. Alaska was the home of more bald eagles than all the other states combined. At least nine nesting pairs were in the Anchorage area. Their favorite food source was fish so that may explain why they lived in an area where there were so many rivers, lakes, and other bodies of water (over 2 million), more water points than in any of the other states, although Minnesota claimed their state to be "The Land of Lakes" on their license plates.

Shortly after leaving Anchorage, we stopped in Palmer at a musk ox farm, just outside of Anchorage. There was an eight-dollar tour for one-half hour that Bob and I chose not to do, but we did learn about musk ox while we were in the gift shop. It is a unique animal found in the arctic regions. Early in Alaska's history, they roamed much of the arctic. After their near extinction, farms helped the musk ox (called 'oomingmak' by the Eskimo) to recover. Many were domesticated. Their fur is eight times warmer by weight than sheep's wool and it does not shrink. It is so very soft and extremely expensive. A lightweight scarf could cost $250. It is all pretty much the same color, grayish-brown, but each Indian tribe has its own pattern. Palmer is located in the Matanuska Valley that is the only agricultural area in Alaska. It is famous for growing huge vegetables, especially cabbages that flourish in the 24 hours of daylight during the summer. They are so proud of their cabbages that the city plants them as part of the landscaping all around town. We had noticed throughout our trip how big and bright all the flowers grew all over Alaska.

Next, we began our travels on the beautiful Glenn Highway along the Matanuska River where there were mountains, valleys, glaciers and wildflowers as well as very steep, winding roads and treacherous driving conditions. The drive through the Chugach Mountains was spectacular, especially when we got our first view of the huge Matanuska Glacier from the highway. It was 27 miles long and four miles wide and had been very stable for the past 400 years. We passed a rockslide where we actually saw the rocks tumbling quickly down the mountainside. The Matanuska River Valley had a variety of wildflowers lining the highway. During that time, we were inundated with mosquitoes, possibly because we were parked right next to a stream! They were teeny tiny and must have been able to penetrate through our screens. That night, we kept awakening to the incessant buzzing and our reactional swatting at those pestilent invaders. It was not a good night's sleep. After about three days of their awful and ceaseless attacks, they finally subsided. We brought mosquito netting with us because we were forewarned that the Alaskan mosquitoes were going to be terrible. Possibly by a stroke of luck, our Alaskan visit came to a close at the end of July, allowing us to miss the full fury of these loathsome predators. Everywhere we had driven through Alaska and British Columbia, there had been wildflowers along both sides of the road, sometimes clumps of white and purple, many yellows, and the purple hues of fireweed (named because it was usually found where soil had been disturbed or where there had been a fire). All the driving, no matter how hazardous had phenomenal scenery.

In an area called the Copper River Valley, named for the 287-mile-long Great Copper River, we traveled from Glennallen on the Glenn Highway to the Richardson Highway that took us all the way to Valdez, where the Alyeska pipeline ends. The pipeline built in Alaska was often referred to as the Alyeska pipeline for the company which operated it. On that excursion to Valdez, it wasn't the destination that was so wonderful, but the trip on the way down. As we headed up toward Thompson Pass, we came to Worthington Glacier, not one of the biggest glaciers, but one that we could walk right up to, very accessible from the road. The scenery at Thompson Pass was stunning. That pass received more snow than anywhere else in Alaska, snow covering the highest jagged mountain peaks that looked like giant shark's teeth. When we came down from Thompson Pass, we followed the Lowe River swollen with milky bluish gray glacier snowmelt through Keystone Canyon. Glacier waters made the water a strange color, and that was how we could tell when rivers were glacier fed. We also passed beaver lodges and dams and huge waterfalls, Bridal Veil Falls and Horsetail Falls, both coming down the canyon at great speeds. Valdez was a small town located in a beautiful setting on Prince William Sound. Thickly forested, snow-capped mountains and 18 glaciers surrounded it. We had learned so much on that trip. It was very educational in addition to being scenic.

On another day, we took the Edgarton Highway, off the Richardson, and went to Chitina, the gateway to the Wrangell-Saint Elias National Park, with 58 miles of unpaved, very rough road. We couldn't go very far into the park without a four-wheel-drive vehicle. Although it was the nation's largest national park, it was very difficult to see any of it, except from the air. Most of the national parks in Alaska were really meant to preserve wildlife and human access was not made easy. They were great for serious hikers. Chitina was a tiny community with a population of 84, several historical buildings, a national park Visitors Center, and the "It'll Do Café" which looked pretty rundown but seemed typical of the Alaskan attitude. We frequently stopped along the road and just stood and marveled at the incredible vastness of the land. On the way back, we saw a moose cow eating from the bottom of the lake, her calf watching, as we also watched. She dipped her head all the way under water and came up with big clumps of vegetation in her mouth to share with her calf.

We next drove to Tok where we had taken Route 2 to Fairbanks at the beginning of our trip. That time when we reached Tok, we took a road north to a town (used loosely) called Chicken because when it was founded the people wanted to name their town after the state bird, ptarmigan, but they couldn't spell it, so they used Chicken instead. Both Chicken and the next town Boundary were primitive, no phone lines, no running water, no electricity, no plumbing. They kept a generator running for power and went to Fairbanks, over 300 miles away, a couple times a month for supplies. It was not too hard to imagine why so few people lived up there. The night we camped near Chicken we were parked next to the South Fork River where we swam and found the water not too cold. Baggins enjoyed the

wading and I liked to lie on my back and just let the current take me down stream. That was the only time we found it warm enough to think about swimming on the entire trip. It was 87 degrees that evening and by the next afternoon the temperature was only 50 degrees.

As we left Alaska and crossed back over into the Yukon Territory, we stopped at another border check. The time changed back into the Pacific Time Zone as we traveled on the Top of the World Highway, a road many people had talked about. It was unpaved, dusty and very bumpy, no shoulders, no center markings, and definitely not worth the trip. We had seen better scenery in many other places. It was not a road we would recommend. It took us to Dawson City, a very touristy-type town, that we certainly could have skipped. There was a little ferry, free of charge, that could only fit a motor home and about six cars on at one time to get into Dawson City. We waited about 45 minutes to get on while we watched parasailers cross the Yukon River.

At that point, the other couple with whom we were traveling wanted to stay in campgrounds. We decided we would rather continue to dry camp the rest of the way to save money, so we split up. We headed back to Whitehorse. No matter which road one took in and out of Alaska, Whitehorse was on the way. We were on the Klondike Highway, named for the old gold-digging territory, and stopped at a wonderful rest area called Five Fingers Rapids just before Carmacks. To avoid the Top of the World Highway and still get to see Five Fingers Rapids, a side trip from Whitehorse would be a more pleasant excursion, evading many dusty bumps in the road. We took a mile hike down a very steep hill to see the Yukon River close up again, being reminded that we had seen it way up north above the Arctic Circle. It was a very long, beautiful river. The Yukon Territory pretty much looked like Alaska.

We were not impressed with the movie at the Visitors Center in Whitehorse. It seemed to be just a movie to get people to come to the Yukon, kind of like an advertisement. We stopped at Bove Island Lake which was named by an American government explorer in 1885, named Schwatka. He wrote a book called *A Summer in Alaska*, which may interest the historian in you. The next explorer who came through was Dawson, a Canadian. From Carcross in the Yukon, we drove to Skagway in Alaska in the car, leaving the motor home at the rest stop where we had spent the night.

Skagway was where the gold rush lived on, in the Historic Gold Rush District. It was a scenic drive from Carcross including a stop at the border. That gave us our 60th and final day in Alaska as we returned to Whitehorse on a road to Watson Lake where we had driven on the trip up. That time, instead of continuing on the Alaska Highway, we took the Cassiar Highway, an alternative route of 446 miles about which we had been cautioned. It was even worse than the warnings -- dirty, dusty, bumpy, winding, hilly, slow, and with lots of construction delays. But it was the only road we could take to get to Stewart, British Columbia and Hyder, Alaska and pass through Bear Glacier and Salmon Glacier where one could actually watch bears catching fish to eat while eagles soared overhead.

On July 25, 2001 we stayed in a campground to power wash the vehicles and take all the tape and plastic off the front of the car and motor home. We had covered the car windshield and the motor home grill in heavy plastic and duct tape when we returned to Whitehorse from Skagway in the car. We did manage to prevent cracking our windshields by driving very slowly. The vehicles were covered in mud, and where the wipers sat were many, many stones from the unpaved roads. The campground was in a perfect setting where there would be no more bad roads. They did not charge for their power wash. We arrived in the early afternoon before there was a line at the power wash so that we could take our time and get both vehicles washed well. We certainly felt blessed not to have had any problems on the roads, especially not to lose a windshield or tire. When we finished, there was a beautiful river beside the campground to walk along into the town across a bridge. Baggins enjoyed that, too. We had spent 12 hours in one day driving on the Cassiar Highway. At one point we drove 75 miles in a 3-1/2 hour period. Everybody needed an afternoon to relax, especially since we planned to dry camp for the rest of the trip. Our original plans were subject to rerouting after we had talked with our youngest son at his summer job at Lake Clear, New York who wanted us to come to his group presentation after their 10-day hiking trip in the wilderness as well as to spend a few days with him. Indeed, our travel plans were substantially modified so we could be able to get to Joshua's camp on time.

As we traveled full time, we had to decide when our Alaska trip ended and when our other travels began again. So we picked the day after we finished coming down the

Cassiar Highway in British Columbia, Canada considering we started our Alaskan advernture when leaving Nevada some 82 days before. To end our Alaska trip notes, we wanted to share that we had 10 overcast/drizzly days, 10 rainy days, 40 sunny and nice days during our 60 days in the State of Alaska. The temperature was less than 65 degrees for 25 days and above 65 degrees for 35 days. We had the best weather in the Kenai Peninsula, always above 70 degrees and not above 78 degrees, always sunny, and featured many wildlife sightings. We saw wildlife on 10 different days while in Alaska and were glad we had seen so much on the trip up because we only saw one grizzly bear between Anchorage and Quebec, with no other sightings of wildlife all the way across Canada. We were very fortunate with only five days of problems with mosquitoes. We never had to wear our mosquito head nets. We were also glad to see darkness when we got back down into Canada. We could see some advantages to having daylight all the time but preferred sleeping in the dark.

We felt like adventurers! We had spent about $2,500 on gasoline, campgrounds, food and attractions to travel about 7,000 miles. We think we might have been able to take a cruise on the Inside Passage to Juneau, the capital city of Alaska (which we missed), rented a small Class C motor home, taken many side trips while in Alaska, and probably come out better cost wise and having been able to see just as much without putting the extensive wear and tear on our vehicles. However, we got to see more of British Columbia the way we travelled and it was certainly beautiful, no doubt about that. All through British Columbia on our way back to the States, we drove beside water and passed city parks, all being so pretty. We also saw quite a bit of logging and many trucks full of huge, long logs. In Prince George, British Columbia, we saw decorative pots of lovely blooming flowers hanging on poles along the streets. We took a detour and stopped in Kelowna, British Columbia to visit with the owners of the park where we had wintered, Lagoons RV Resort in Texas. We learned that British Columbia produced the world's largest supply of ginseng and we saw lots of it covered over with black tarps that let light in.

As blessed as we had been with our vehicles that year, we started having some problems with the motor home and stopped in British Columbia to have front and back brakes put on, to get an oil change and have a universal joint replaced. Previously when it got so sunny that the engine air-conditioner wouldn't cool down the inside of the motor home, we would put on the outside generator in order to use the rooftop air-conditioners. When the generator stopped working, the engine air-conditioners couldn't keep up with the outside heat so we became very hot. We found out later that all of the motor home problems were caused by the terribly rough driving conditions on the Alaska and Cassiar Highways. Both circuit boards in the refrigerator and in the generator had to be replaced as well as the entire frame underneath the motor home.

Other travelers had said there was nothing much to see along the Trans-Canada Highway, and they were pretty much right. There were lots of grain fields. In Revelstoke, we saw a train going through three tunnels through the mountains next to Route 1. We had fun on the CB talking to a trucker who gave us lots of interesting information, should we return to that area when we had more time to sightsee.

We had lots of rain as we drove through Canada's Glacier National Park, part of the Columbia Mountains. We went through Rogers Pass which, when built, was backed up by the world's largest avalanche-control system. (The locals said it rained four out of three days there!) As we crossed into Alberta, we passed the most unusual spiral tunnel for trains in Yoho National Park. We were surprised to find the beautiful areas surrounding Lake Louise, "the gem of the Rockies" not busy with tourists. It was a very small lake with a glacier above it and a chateau hotel built in 1924 on the lake that charged about $550 per room. As with grocery store labels, all signs were in both English and French.

Just before we reached Banff, Alberta a big rainbow was right in front of us. We saw lots more hitchhikers in Canada than we were used to seeing in the United States. We continued to see signs to watch out for moose but we didn't see any moose while we were going east through Canada. In Banff, the central point of the Canadian Rockies, we stopped to see the Banff Springs Hotel with its Victorian architecture and 578 rooms at $800 per night. When it opened it was the world's largest hotel. The rest stops where we spent the night dry camping were like mini-state parks, very private and set far back from the road we were traveling on. That was a great way to save money and still enjoy nature. Despite the air conditioning problems we did for the most part enjoy our dry camping in Canada.

We drove around Calgary and through Medicine Hat, Alberta where there was a nice Visitors Center with a dumpsite. That was important when we were doing so much dry camping. We crossed into Saskatchewan and found lots more flat farmland and sweeping grain fields. We passed huge Reed Lake. In Manitoba, we saw blue flowers in the fields that looked like water in the distance, just beautiful. We listened to a radio station that played vampire music, very strange, we thought. There were lots of fruit stands. Everywhere we looked, hay was rolled up, even in the median strips.

Going through Ontario with scenery much like British Columbia, there were evergreen trees all along the side of the road. After Thunder Bay, on Route 11, we were on The Terry Fox Memorial Highway, named for a young man with cancer who began a run across Canada on one leg. Ontario graced us with a beautiful red sunset as we drove. We saw a sign to usher in the town of Latchford, sitting near a dam, "The best little town by a dam site!" After North Bay, we didn't go into Quebec, but followed right along the border, almost to Ottawa, the capital of Canada, in the Province of Quebec. The television channel CTV had shows from ABC, CBS and NBC all in one night, on the same channel. We also had the pleasure of seeing *West Wing* in French.

We crossed into the United States from the Quebec's Cornwall border into Malone, New York. It had taken us 12 days from the Yukon Territory to get to see our son by the time his camp group was returning from the wilderness. Their presentation was worth the hurried trip across Canada and although we were very tired, we had time while dry camping in the camp's parking lot to relax during the five days we stayed there. They fed us well. We met some other parents who were also visiting and went out to meals with their families, had a nice Sunday morning church service outside under the trees and got some laundry done. Joshua took us on a tour of Camp LaVida including the ropes courses. He took us on a hike up to Owl's Head to see the mountain where the campers do their rock climbing. It was quite an intriguing view from the top of Pitch-Off Mountain. By the time we left there, we had learned quite a bit about what Joshua did during his summers at Lake Clear in the Adirondacks. It was certainly wonderful to have the time to spend with him, one of the benefits of full-time travel. (We didn't know at the time and neither did Joshua that he had become friendly during that wilderness trip with the young lady who would become his wife, and we met Christen that weekend. It was at Owl's Head that he later proposed to her.)

Further south in the Adirondacks, we stopped in Caroga Lake to see friends from Lagoons where we played bridge and then tried two sports neither of us had done before: tubing behind a motor boat and kayaking. On the way back to our campground, we found a lobster dinner for $7.50. We thought it was our lucky day until we discovered that because of tornado warnings, heavy rain, wind, and lightning, our campground had been evacuated. So we had to wait out the storm in the park's large parking lot, away from trees.

We had the opportunity to drive through and around Albany, New York's capital on our way to visit college friends in Livingston, New Jersey. Then we visited my aunt and cousins in another part of New Jersey before heading to a campground in the southern part of the state. The thunderstorms on the Garden State Parkway were so bad that the road's shoulders were full of cars that had pulled off to wait for a break in the torrential downpour. We had a chance to see our son Rob's new house in Vineland, New Jersey. He bought the house under the teachers-next-door program and we had not seen it since he had it all fixed up. In town, it was very large with a nice yard and big garage. He is our oldest son, the one who was adopted and had been fortunate to

have had benefited from several programs for minorities. The teachers-next-door program enabled him to buy a fixer-upper very reasonably with a low-interest mortgage that included enough money for repairs.

We had a perfect beach day in Atlantic City, New Jersey and spent time with two other sons, John and Arn, playing golf and being treated to a ride on their new boat and to a delicious dinner with shrimp-kabobs and a luscious salad which Arn fixed at his new townhouse in Marlton, New Jersey.

We spent a week re-organizing the motor home in Reisterstown, Maryland, our hometown. Bob got an unexpected "perfect" job, working as a consultant for his former boss from 30 years ago. His time was his own, as he visited various architects in Baltimore, Washington, DC and surrounding areas, telling them about library furnishings. While Bob worked from Reisterstown, we moved the motor home to Spring Grove, Pennsylvania where I stayed to help our granddaughter's mom with babysitting. She drove a dump truck and left for work at 5:30 in the morning, so I was there the first day of school and for three months to put Ashley, then age nine, on the school bus and be there when she returned from school to help with schoolwork. We had a lot of fun times together and she got to see her Granddad on the weekends. During the week he stayed in a condo that my mom had lived in until she died. It had been rented but was currently vacant, which made for a very workable situation. Being all week long without a car and being in the country not within walking distance of a store was a different lifestyle, one that I enjoyed for the time I was there. Ashley's teacher told us that we had benefited Ashley in getting her caught up to her class level academically, so we were glad we had been able to help. On weekends we were able to visit with many old friends and see more of our children, too.

On that horrible day of September 11th, it happened that it was a school holiday for Ashley. We took her with us to Robin and Eric's house in Union Bridge, Maryland to babysit for our newest granddaughter, Danielle. At about 11 o'clock in the morning, a woman next door to where we were sitting outside, screamed to me about why I was sitting calmly and told me to go inside and turn on the television. What a shock that was! It was one of those times like when President John F. Kennedy had been shot, a day everyone will remember for the rest of his life, where he was and what he was doing that day.

Cal Ripken, a Baltimore Oriole baseball player, decided to retire and we were lucky enough to be present for his last career game, coincidentally on my birthday. We had always enjoyed attending games in Oriole Park at Camden Yards. Being there again at that special time was awesome for us. Since opening in 1992, our hometown ballpark had become one of the most influential in baseball. Many other stadiums had since been built with a similar design. My cousin had won the bid to put in all the molding to renovate the 1898 B & O Warehouse, eight stories high, several blocks long, located beyond the seats in right field. Besides all the food spots inside the stadium, as we entered between the seats and the warehouse were stands to buy ribs and barbeques. The seats were all green and in the many times we frequented the ballpark, we always enjoyed our seats from various positions and loved the way the seats were nestled below street level, giving a wonderful view of Baltimore City behind center field. No matter where we sat, we had the feeling that we were very close to the field.

On a sadder note, because we had stayed in the area for three months to babysit for Ashley, we were available to attend two funerals of family members and also get to see the older members of both of our families. That reminded us why we had sold our home in 1998 and decided to travel full time while we could. Bob's temporary boss unexpectedly invited us to Thanksgiving dinner at his home. The next day we met Rob, John, Arn and Joshua, four of our sons for lunch in Wilmington, Delaware. We felt very blessed when we got to see all of the children during the year and especially fortunate having so many of them together at one time.

When we lived in the Baltimore, Maryland area it was seldom that we had time for sightseeing in our own backyard. We went downtown into Baltimore one night for the Christmas lighting of the Washington Monument and to visit Walter's Art Gallery where we had never been although we both had grown up in that area. The Washington Monument in Baltimore was the first monument ever put up to honor our first president.

The time we spent in Spring Grove, Pennsylvania and Reisterstown, Maryland was a rewarding time for us, and then it was time to move on in order to be in the warm weather of Rockport, Texas for the winter. Our motor home didn't like the cold weather. We took about eight days to make the trip and traveled through Lexington, Virginia, Kodak and Yuma, Tennessee, Hot Springs, Arkansas, Tyler and Houston, Texas. We thoroughly enjoyed our two-day stay in Hot Springs National Park, the only national park in an urban area. We took advantage of the bathhouses in Hot

Springs. There used to be many, many bathhouses there. It was a famous vacation spot at the beginning of the century before penicillin was discovered. People came from all over the world to experience the healing effects of the mineral waters. There was only one still functioning and we enjoyed finding out what it had been like. We arrived in Rockport for the Christmas season and a visit from Joshua and his girlfriend. So the year ended much as it had begun, at Lagoons RV Resort with Joshua and lots of other friends we took pleasure in seeing each winter.

*"More time, more satisfaction -
it's within us all,
and it was there all the time."*

— From *A Thousand Paths To A Peaceful Life*

by David Baird

Chapter Seven

Our Fifth Year - Presidential Homes and More

Our Journey in 2002

From Texas through Louisiana to Florida,
Maryland through Colorado to Nevada

When we picked Joshua and Christen up at the Corpus Christi airport, it was interesting to see the changes in increased security after the September 11th terrorism. It was fun having them visit and getting to greet the New Year with them. Besides the many activities that we continued to participate in at Lagoons RV Resort and doing our workcamping chores, we did some sightseeing around the Rockport, Texas area that we had not done before. We attended the South Texas Opry in Corpus Christi, took a 16-mile bike ride through the Aransas National Wildlife Refuge with friends we had met in Americus, Georgia (who came to Rockport to work on a Habitat house), toured the USS Lexington and the Fulton Mansion with college friends who visited from Michigan, went to the Rockport Center for the Arts, drove by many bent live oak trees. They are an unusual sight. The gusty winds in the area had caused all the trees to bend. We went to Goose Island State Park to see the Big Tree, the biggest and best of the live oak trees. It was at least 1,000 years old, 35 feet in circumference, 11 feet in diameter, and 44 feet high. It was surrounded by Anchor fencing to keep it protected. We had previously mentioned that Rockport was a birding paradise. That year we took a whooping crane boat tour to see those beautiful and large white birds with long necks that had become nearly extinct. The Fulton Beach area of Rockport was the winter home to the migratory whooping cranes, and until recently, the only southern habitat for those birds.

During the three months we were in Rockport, in addition to workcamping duties at Lagoons, Bob continued to work for the Maryland firm through phone, fax, and e-mail use. Rockport had no local number for Juno or AOL, so we paid for phone service and for Internet service in order for Bob to keep up with his architectural contacts. I continued to offer bridge lessons to anyone in the community. There was no charge and we had about 30 players, learning, getting refreshed, or helping to teach at various levels.

After participating in a bridge tournament on March 16th, we left Rockport in the late afternoon for San Antonio where we spent the night at a Walmart parking lot for our first time. Many RVers stayed at Walmart because it was free and very convenient for shopping. We arrived late at night so it seemed opportune for us to stay there instead of hunting for a campground in the dark. The parking lots in Walmart were big enough to maneuver a motor home. All through the night, a security vehicle kept us safe. In the morning we attended Max Lucado's Oak Hills Church of Christ but he wasn't there. I had read some of his books so had looked forward to meeting him. That was the reason we went to San Antonio. We stopped at Lake Conroe in Texas for a few days, then on to Lafayette, Louisiana where we stayed long enough to try out two restaurants that friends had recommended for crawfish. Then we went through Baton Rouge where we saw such a tall Capitol building on exceptionally landscaped and manicured grounds that we were glad we had made that stop. In front of the Capitol were 48 steps going across, each labeled with a state's name. We thought that was neat.

To get to New Orleans, Louisiana we crossed the 23-mile Causeway Bridge over Lake Ponchatrain just as the sun was setting, red on the horizon. For his birthday, we ate at Bob's favorite place in New Orleans for raw oysters - Felix's. He won't eat them any place else any more because of the possibility of contamination. It was always an unusual and fun experience to visit New Orleans. We drove right along the beaches of pretty white sand on the Gulf of Mexico in Southern Mississippi. The Cajun people in that area called themselves Acadians. The USS Alabama, a 35,000-ton World War II battleship was decommissioned at the Puget Sound Navy Yard in 1947. Since 1964, she had been stationed in Mobile, Alabama as a memorial to World War II veterans. We crossed another causeway across the Mobile Bay.

While in Florida for a couple of weeks, we visited eight different couples who had moved to Florida from various parts of the country. It was fun seeing all the varied lifestyles people our age chose. We were certainly happy doing what we were doing, seeing so much of our country and meeting so many nice people and getting better acquainted with old friends and relatives. We also toured the Tampa Bay Devil Rays Tropicana Field in St. Petersburg, Florida. That stadium was the last one at that time to be built with a dome, chosen because of all the rain in that area. It had Field Turf, which was plastic grass instead of natural grass because grass was hard to grow under a dome. Entering the Tropicana Field was like going through the Rotunda years ago at Brooklyn's Ebbets Field, a flash of past baseball. The seats were all in bright blue. In an area above the lower level in left field was a section with beach décor and tropical foliage which seemed to give the field its name. We were told about interesting plays off the outfield wall because of the nooks and crannies in the wall. When we toured a park, we enjoyed having the guide take our picture in the dugout.

When we got into South Carolina, we had a reunion with the couple who had sold us the motor home five years before and had since moved to Hilton Head, South Carolina. Then we spent a few days in Virginia Beach, Virginia where I signed up to workcamp during July and August.

When we got to Reisterstown, Maryland again we parked the motor home in the parking lot where our condo was. We were able to keep it there for a while because we helped out the Condominium Association in various ways. We got involved that year in planning a clean-up day. We attended meetings and gave the Association our manual labor to get some things repaired and planted. We weren't there long when I heard that my friend in North Jersey was having a serious pancreas operation and needed some help at home, so I went up there for a week while Bob borrowed a car from our daughter, Robin. When I returned we had the opportunity to help Robin and her husband, Eric with their daughter, Danielle move from a house they had been renting to an older, big home in the same town of Union Bridge, Maryland.

In 2001, we had attended Cal Ripken's last baseball game. In early May of 2002, we got to meet Cal Ripken and his wife, Kelly. We got his autograph and shook hands with him and took pictures. We had gone into Baltimore to see *The Season* about Cal Ripken's last season with lots of playbacks of his career. He was the first baseball player to wear a wire during his entire last season, including spring training, so that his every movement and word would be captured on tape. The movie included footage of his family, Kelly, Rachel and Ryan, traveling with him to the away games and Ryan, age seven, was the Orioles bat boy during that last season. After the movie, there was a question and answer session with the filmmaker and the Ripkens. We thought that in 50 years from then, having seen Cal Ripken would be just like having met Babe Ruth. It was very exciting for baseball fans.

In mid-May we took the motor home and our granddaughter, Ashley up to Massachusetts where our youngest son graduated from Gordon College in Wenham. It was a fun time being with the family at such an auspicious time, although pouring rain kept the ceremony from being held outside. Bob continued to work in Maryland for the company he had been working for while we were in Texas. His summer hours were very flexible so that he was able to come to Virginia Beach each weekend while I workcamped there. Before we left for Virginia, we did a Habitat project in South Bend, Indiana with the Notre Dame alumni and Bob was the house leader again for the third year. That was the 10th Habitat project we had been involved in during the five years we had been on the road. Each one was something special. Many of the same volunteers were with us again that year. A new program was started so that a few of the Notre Dame alumni brought their 17-year-old daughters and sons with them. Bob particularly enjoyed getting them initiated. Our homeowner, Mary was outside with us everyday and so very grateful to each and every one of us. She made a point of talking to each of us individually and getting to learn about our families. I got to be sure that everyone was fed snacks and lunches and that each person consumed plenty of water while Bob made sure that everyone felt needed and had the opportunity to learn new skills. We ended the week singing one of Habitat's favorites, *"On Holy Ground"*. It had been another satisfying, rewarding, and blessed week for us all.

We did some visiting on the way and then left the motor home in South Bend because we had put it in a frame shop when we got there and it wasn't ready when we finished building our Habitat house. It took them two weeks and we felt lucky that we got it back then because the frame was shot and they had to replace a lot of metal and do a lot of welding. It was a big job and it was hard to believe that our insurance company picked up the $4,000 bill because they determined that it was caused by the road hazards in Alaska the summer before. We had been trying to find a shop to repair it in Canada, Texas, Florida, and Maryland, and no one could determine what was wrong. The Holiday Rambler factory suggested that place in South Bend that was coincidentally where we were going in June anyway. We stayed with our Michigan friends while the mechanics worked on the motor home. It was unbelievably hot in Michigan, as it was across most of the United States that summer. We were introduced to Cabella's Sporting Goods store with its ostrich, caribou and bison sandwiches, along with many interesting displays. We toured the Gerald Ford Presidential Library in Ann Arbor. There was an entry hall with plaques on the wall. Otherwise, there wasn't much to see. As in most of the presidential libraries, the papers were hidden from public view.

We also took a side trip to the Chicago, Illinois area to visit Bob's sister and family there, before heading back to pick up the motor home in Indiana.

At six o'clock in the evening the motor home wasn't ready so we went to see the Habitat women's build in South Bend. The first time we had experienced a women's build was when Hillary Clinton had come to Georgia to help Rosalynn Carter and other first ladies (women governors and mayors or wives of such) build a house with only women volunteers. We learned that a woman working on the house in South Bend had accidentally walked off the roof and had been hospitalized but would be okay. Their house was coming along fine. We had worked with their house leader on our Notre Dame build the week before. We finally left South Bend with our motor home at nearly midnight and parked shortly after that at a rest area on the Indiana/Ohio border. We were glad to get settled in for the night in what felt like a new motor home.

While we were in Virginia Beach we were able to enjoy the ocean only two miles from the campground, a quick 10-minute drive, and the water was clear, no jellyfish, no seaweed, and such a great temperature. We were big ocean and beach fans, having been brought up on the East Coast. It was amazing how breezy and cool it was on the beach when it was so brutally hot at the campground. Being bridge fans, we put up a  sign in the windshield about wanting to play "relaxed" bridge. A couple stopped by and we enjoyed playing with them often. Our son, John came to visit and we did some sightseeing in the area, visiting the Battleship Wisconsin and the MacArthur Memorial in Norfolk, Virginia. That was during the weekends when Bob came to stay. During the week my workcamping duties included cleaning the five big bathhouses. It was extremely hot work that summer with temperatures outside in the 100s and even higher temperatures inside the bathhouses. I was glad that I could swim in the afternoons when the work was finished.

After leaving Virginia Beach, we visited Monticello, President Thomas Jefferson's home and Ash-Lawn, President James Monroe's home and Michie's Tavern, and drove passed the golden dome Capitol building in Charleston, West Virginia on the Kanawha River. We enjoyed various billboards on our travels. One in West Virginia said, "Will the road you're on take you to my place?" Another said, "If you're looking for a sign from God, here it is." Then we saw the huge mansion and gardens of the Kingswood Center that was opened to the public when Charles Kelly King donated his estate, just absolutely eloquent, in Lucas, Ohio where we also visited friends from Lagoons RV Resort. We visited the Living Bible Museum and had a ride on a carousel that was in the middle of Lucas.

After we left Ohio, we stopped to see Bob's aunt in Pittsburgh and got into the Pittsburgh Pirates PNC Park. It was a new baseball stadium although it had been built on the same site as the old one. We were allowed to walk around the inside without having to pay for a tour. We had found no uniformity in visiting baseball parks. Not all had tours. Some only allowed us in if we purchased a ticket for a game. A few, like the one in Pittsburgh, permitted us inside to take pictures without a charge. The Pirates ballpark used to be called Three Rivers Stadium because it was on a site where the Ohio, Allegheny and the Monongahela Rivers all came together.

Many states in the East were in terrible drought conditions during the summer and fall of 2002. In Frederick, Maryland if they hadn't finally gotten some rain, they were going to have to buy water. People had been collecting their shower water in buckets to flush their toilets. Late in October, we had 48 hours of steady, glorious rain. And then we had another day of it after a short break. Believe me, no one complained! Things actually began to turn green again, just in time for the leaves to fall! That gave area residents hope for the following spring. Bob decided to continue working in the Maryland area through October so we had the opportunity to attend a few birthday parties for several relatives and celebrate mine with a visit from Joshua and Christen. We spent more time with Robin, Eric and our granddaughter, Danielle.

Bob also turned some of his business outings into sightseeing. We went to Annapolis, the capital city of Maryland where we toured the Capitol building, attended the year-anniversary Mass for 9/11/01, and saw the tomb of John Paul Jones at the Naval Academy. We toured the Ripken Stadium in Aberdeen, Maryland. We had lunch on the water in Havre De Grace, Maryland. We attended a wonderful evening program at Fort McHenry in Baltimore that had been held every year since the War of 1812, an example of one of the many places to visit in our hometown area, which we had not been aware of when we lived there. We did some sightseeing with friends to Harper's Ferry, West Virginia where John Brown had been killed before the Civil War. We also went to the Baltimore National Aquarium, and to Washington, DC to see Mount Vernon, President George Washington's home.

The sniper(s) that plagued the Maryland, Virginia, and DC areas started out about 40 minutes from us. There was attention all over the country paid to that. Bob and I had spent some time that summer reading about serial killers, among other subjects. The snipers began on October 2, 2002 and after killing 10 people they were apprehended on October 24, 2002, about three weeks later. It was a relief to have them caught.

Just before we left Maryland for the winter, we went out with friends to eat the famous Chesapeake Bay blue crabs. Those were a treat with which both Bob and I grew up. Our families could purchase the live crabs from vendors along the street for a couple of dollars per dozen. We would sit outside and cook them in big pots over coals with Old Bay spice made locally in Baltimore. Everyone would sit around picnic tables covered with newspaper and eat them by the dozen, maybe with a beer and some potato salad. The night we bought them to eat in a restaurant, we paid $65 per dozen. Prices had changed but the crabs were still as good as we remembered them.

On the way to Pahrump, Nevada we stopped to see five couples whom we knew from our winters in Texas. It was good to see them since we wouldn't be going to Texas that year. We did a little sightseeing in Hannibal, Missouri, the home of Mark Twain, then visited the Dwight David Eisenhower Center in Abilene, Kansas which included the presidential library and his home. There was much pretty, brownish marble throughout the library. A huge painting of the White House with all the presidents from Washington to Eisenhower, each in the fashion of their day standing on the front lawn, was hanging in public view. The magnitude of the portrait was just awesome.

We traveled on Route 70, a route we had not taken all the way across the United States before. It went through Vale Pass at 10,600 feet high and followed along the White River. The way the rocks were held back by stone walls covered with screening was fascinating. We tried to vary our course as much as we could. It was an 11-day trip with lots of different weather conditions. We started with two days of rain. It was cold pretty much the whole way across. We found the Red Rock Amphitheatre, a tremendous quirk of nature, in the Denver, Colorado area. We awakened in Denver to a snowstorm with lots of snow on the ground, but after church the roads seemed clear enough, so we left in mid-morning. Up and down the mountains we saw overturned  vehicles and those that had skidded off the roadways. It was scary but Bob's good driving kept us safe. We kept going because we wanted to get to Preferred RV Resort in Pahrump, Nevada by Thanksgiving. We went slowly and drove longer that day than we were used to. Then the next day in Utah we hit some terrible winds that tried to sway the motor home, so we stopped about four o'clock and were glad we did. I didn't think I had ever felt wind like that. The next morning all was well and by the time we hit Las Vegas, it was sunny, warm, and wonderful. Pahrump was just a little over an hour from Las Vegas and only 20 minutes from the California border.

It was fun to be back at Preferred RV Resort where we had stayed before but we hadn't spent an entire winter there. Different people came there at various times of the year. Some liked the cooler temperatures than further south. Some came in the fall or spring on their way down or back from warmer areas. Few chose to stay in the desert during the summer months. We had an opportunity to help put up Christmas decorations as well as to volunteer to transport persons from Pahrump to the Las Vegas hospital. We both taught bridge lessons to beginners and made several trips to visit our granddaughter, Ashley who was living with her parents in Henderson, Nevada at that time.

Baggins and I walked for hours in the desert. The mountains that we saw everyday from the desert were covered with snow where the skiing was on Mount Charleston. The mountains that surrounded the area were always changing color and always beautiful. Even though the rest of the area was very dried out looking, we understood why so many people had been moving to Pahrump. The city is located over one of the largest aquifers in the country. The mountains were ever present and the weather during our winter there was fantastic. We had only three days of rain during our three-month stay. Every afternoon, even when the night and early morning hours got down to the low 40s, the sun shone brightly and a sweatshirt was enough. The afternoon temperatures were usually in the mid-70s and the sun made that seem even warmer. We surely liked being in the warmer climates during our winters. We spent Christmas with our friends there, missing all of our family members. That was the first year we hadn't been with our youngest son, Joshua sometime during the holidays because he didn't have school vacations any more and would have had to take time off from work. Neither of us could afford plane tickets. During that holiday, we were treated at one of the casinos to a wonderfully scrumptious strawberry shortcake dessert served in a huge glass on a stem, like a brandy snifter with a huge bowl and served with two spoons. It was the biggest dessert we had ever seen and a delicious way to celebrate our wedding anniversary and to end the year of 2002.

*"It's not where or when you arrive -
it's taking the journey
that counts."*

— Anonymous

Chapter Eight

Our Sixth Year

The End of Full-Time RVing and the Beginning of Long Trips

Our Journey in 2003

**From Nevada to California, Arizona and Texas to Maryland,
New York through Maine to the Canadian Maritime Provinces,
Quebec to New Jersey and Maryland to the Florida Keys**

We started the New Year 2003 with a side trip from Pahrump, Nevada on New Year's Eve to go to Pasadena, California to see the Rose Parade. We met a couple who took us to the parade and showed us where to park and where to sit, making the logistics much easier. We had originally thought that the only way we could see the parade was by taking our motor home to one of the areas where we could park it and sit on top of it, but discovered that the cost for that was too prohibitive for us and as it turned out, we saw everything just fine without spending a penny. We sat about six rows back from the parade on our chairs. The people in front of us stayed seated so we could, too. Most everybody around us was standing, but we could see fine from our chairs. There weren't as many people as they had expected but it looked like an awful lot to us. There were about 100 entries in the parade, about 50 of them were floats, and the rest were bands and horses mostly. We sat for about three hours in the luscious California sunshine and it was fun.

Another day, we visited Forest Lawn Cemetery in Glendale that was actually built for the living. Mr. Eaton, Forest Lawn's founder had the idea that the cemetery should be a place not of grief but of serenity. Before Word War II, he had gone to Santa Maria delle Grazie to see Leonardo DaVinci's Last Supper masterpiece and because he was afraid it would be destroyed by time, he commissioned Signora Rosa Caselli-Moretti, a descendent of an ancient family of Peruvian artists, to make a stained-glass reproduction. He wanted it not to look the way it did when he saw it at Saint Marie delle Grazie but the way he supposed it to have looked when DaVinci painted it. That stained-glass window of DaVinci's Last Supper is located in Forest Lawn's special building called the Great Mausoleum and built just for the purpose to house the enormous-sized window (30 feet wide and 15 feet high). It also houses the grave of Gutzon Borglam, the sculptor who carved Mount Rushmore, among others. Then another building was built to house the largest religious painting in America, called the Crucifixion (195 feet wide and 45 feet high), painted by Polish artist Jan Styka. It is the largest framed-mounted-to-canvas painting in the world. Both are astounding sights!

When we left Pasadena, California we stayed in a state park on the ocean in Ventura. While in Ventura, we took a boat trip to the Channel Islands National Park and had a beautiful, sunny ride on a catamaran, and awed by our first contact with gray as well as grampus whales and dolphins as we took time for whale watching. It was a half-day trip and very pleasant. Unless they were going to backpack on the islands, most boaters were not allowed to get onto the islands but we got very close. Then we went to see Dodger Stadium in Los Angeles and it instantly became our favorite baseball park. It had such a picturesque view of the mountains from almost any seat in the park. There were five seating decks with multi-colored seats, a new video board in left field, and newly installed out-of-town scoreboards on both fences in left and right fields. Although it was an older park, it was clean and well kept, getting painted every year. We look forward to someday being able to see a game played there.

We had time for Bob to continue his quest to see the presidential libraries. There were two in Southern California. The Richard Nixon Library and birthplace were in Yorba Linda with exhibits about the 30th president of the United States. The Ronald Reagan Library in Simi Valley was impressive. The long street leading to the library was lined with flags of all the presidents. We saw the sunset from the part of the Berlin Wall that was in the back of the Reagan Library. The library featured the 40th president's Hollywood years as well as his political career, including his years as governor of California from 1967 to 1974 and the assassination attempt by John W. Hinckley, Jr.

We had been to San Diego previously and always enjoyed going back there. The campground had an outside heated pool and spa, and a great dog run where Baggins could run unleashed. That was unusual for any campground. We weren't there much, as we spent the four days sightseeing and enjoying weather in the 80s. We also had some Santa Anna winds. We went to the current Padres Qualcomm Stadium but weren't allowed to see the field because it was going to be used for the Super Bowl and they were afraid of terrorist activity. The San Diego Chargers football team also used that field. It was disappointing not to get inside the stadium, but we got to see the new Padres stadium to be called Petco Park, under construction, similar to the way Oriole Park at Camden Yards was positioned in the city of Baltimore.

We also went to Balboa Park, a cultural center and viewed the Lewis and Clark expedition at the IMAX Theatre. The architecture at the park was wonderful, lots of history there. We saw a 200-foot tower with a 100-bell carillon. There was a big Visitors Center hospitality room and a huge set up of model trains. An organ was situated in an outside amphitheatre. We took Baggins to Ocean Beach where part of it was a dog beach and the dogs could run unleashed. California seemed to be quite dog friendly. We also took a particularly scenic drive on Silver Strand Boulevard between the Pacific Ocean and the San Diego Bay, although all the driving in the Southern California area was picturesque. We enjoyed ourselves and headed back on a two-day trip through the Mohave Desert in order to return to Pahrump. The Mohave Desert is part of the San Bernardino National Forest and a good place for Baggins to run free. The route we took back to Pahrump was very mountainous. Route 138 was steep, very winding, and paved with red material. The mountains alongside of us looked burned with black bushes, not green. Our brakes were very smelly when we got off Route 138, but the views were beautiful.

We got involved in many activities at Preferred RV Resort. While I taught bridge Bob kept busy on the computer, continuing to work as a library consultant for his old firm. We learned that Pahrump had a population of about 28,000 and was one of the fastest growing cities in our nation. In 1963, there was no electricity there and no phones until 1965. When we first went there in 1998, there was one major casino. In 2003, there were five major casinos and more RV parks. There was still no Walmart but it was planned for the near future. For serious shopping, one had to go into Las Vegas about 1-1/4 hours away. The people in Pahrump referred to Las Vegas as "going into town".

On February first when the Space Shuttle Columbia explosion occurred, I was on my way to pick up Bob at Las Vegas' McCarran International Airport. He hadn't heard about the explosion. He had been to Maryland to work at his office for about 10 days, making us money to keep us keeping on! We learned how different airport security was since 9/11. We hadn't realized that I wouldn't be able to meet him at the gate and hadn't made plans for where else to meet, so it took us a while before we caught up to each other.

We left Pahrump, Nevada on February 19th and returned to Reisterstown, Maryland on Bob's birthday, March 31st, a jaunt of six weeks with lots of visiting and sightseeing, new roads, and a newer motor home. From Pahrump, we first headed north so that Bob could go skiing at Lake Tahoe on Mount Rose at an elevation of 8,900 feet. Then we drove around Lake Tahoe through Carson City, the capital of Nevada. Although we had been in the Northern California area before, we had not gone to Lake Tahoe. We toured San Francisco on a beautiful day. It is a city of many bridges. San Francisco Bay Bridge is stacked and goes through a tunnel on Treasure Island. The Third Street Bridge is near Pacific Bell Park, the home of the San Francisco Giants baseball team. There we walked around the park without having to pay for a tour. It is right on the water. The baseball park is located in the China Basin area in downtown San Francisco. At the main entrance is a wonderful statue of Willie Mays. Also outside are two tall clock towers with pyramid-shaped roofs, topped by flagpoles. The main three-tiered grandstand consists of green seats. No seats are beyond the right field wall because of McCovey Cove, part of the San Francisco Bay, giving fans a great view. The world's largest baseball glove and four slides inside a giant Coca-Cola bottle are part of a play area which could be seen from anywhere in the stadium.

We could see the Golden Gate Bridge and Alcatraz Island from Fisherman's Wharf on San Francisco Bay. Alcatraz, also called The Rock, where many notorious criminals had been held during its operation as America's maximum-security prison from the 1930s until the 1960s, is a popular tourist attraction. Back in Nevada, we visited Reno, another place we had never been before. In Reno we parked in one of the casino parking lots, not glamorous but free.

We stayed in Lone Pine, California heading south again, near Mount Whitney that is the highest peak in the continental United States. Our next stop was at Quartzsite, Arizona where we stayed in the desert dry camping, something we had not done before. Baggins ran free all over the desert area where we were parked. Apparently many campers stopped in Quartzsite for the flea markets that lined the streets in January and February. By the time we went through, however, many of the booths were gone.

We spent 10 days in Phoenix, parked in front of our friend's house. It wasn't yet baseball season when we arrived, so we took a tour of the Arizona Diamondbacks Bank One Ballpark, known as The BOB. The identifying feature of that ballpark was its combination of a retractable roof, air conditioning, and a natural turf field. Nearby in Peoria, Arizona was where we traded in our 35-foot 1989 for a 35-foot 1999 Holiday Rambler with a slide-out, so our living space got a little larger, although our storage inside was a little smaller. We adjusted to the changes nicely. A slide-out in a motor home or trailer was a part of the wall that slid out from the aisle so that there was more floor space when we were parked. In our 1999 Holiday Rambler, the slide-out allowed the living room and kitchen areas to become more spacious. A slide-out might be 18 inches wide or wider. Ours was the smaller one. The slide-out could only be moved when the rig was not moving. From the outside while we were moving, one couldn't tell there was anything different. That was a new addition to RVs about 1996. So when we were originally looking for a used motor home, there were no used slide-out versions available.

We had been trying to sell our 1989 Holiday Rambler on the Internet for almost a year. When we realized that it had 150,000 miles on it, was 14 years old (even though we had recently updated many features) and probably would not be easy to sell on our own, we decided to trade it in. We also were in a different financial situation than we had been in 1997 when we had bought our first one. We had cash then. By 2003, we had spent our cash traveling. If we had been able to sell our old motor home first and then had time to look for a replacement, we might have been able to work it out financially, but because we were living in it, it would have been difficult to unload it and take time to find a newer one. However, we were headed back to Maryland where Bob was going to continue to work. We were going to have to give up our full-time RVing lifestyle. Having Bob back to work meant that we could afford payments if we traded in our old motor home to upgrade. So that was what we did.

We stopped in Tucson, Arizona where we stayed in Saguaro National Park, such a lovely sight, all varieties of cacti everywhere. We went to De Grazia's Gallery in the Sun and met an artist there and marveled at De Grazia's work in so many mediums on various subjects. We found a room in which the Stations of the Cross, painted by him, were narrated and as it happened to be Ash Wednesday, the timing was perfect to stay for that. Fifty-one miles into New Mexico, we crossed the Continental Divide. Next, we camped in Pancho Villa, a historical site, designated as the last place raided by Mexico in the United States in 1916. (Until 9/11/01, no foreign power had attacked us on our mainland.) That was in Columbus, New Mexico near the border so that we could cross over into Mexico at Polomas for prescriptions, eyeglasses, dental work and some great

Mexican food. Then we went up to Los Lunas, New Mexico where we had started our journey in 1997, to visit my aunt and uncle. It was a little out of our way, so we parked the motor home and drove further north in the car. There is a historical marker in San Antonio, New Mexico where Conrad Hilton was born and had built his first hotel. He had asked my aunt to marry him long before he was wealthy and she had turned him down! We stopped to see where Billy the Kid escaped from the County Courthouse in Lincoln, New Mexico.

In Noodle, Texas we parked at the house of a high school friend, way out in the country and Baggins enjoyed that freedom a lot. My friend lived by herself on 132 acres and there was nothing to be seen from her house except land. At night it was kind of spooky being in the middle of absolutely nowhere with no lights anywhere around. We stopped to visit friends from Lagoons in Abilene on our way to Dallas, Texas to see the spot where President John F. Kennedy had been shot. The Book Depository has a museum in his honor near that site. In the Biblical Arts Center, there is a mural of the Pentecost, which is 50 days after Passover, one of the largest murals in the world. Every time we went through Texas, we realized how huge that state is.

We drove through Little Rock, the capital city of Arkansas and stopped at the Capitol building. We also rode by the site for the new William J. Clinton Presidential Library in Little Rock that at that time had been scheduled to be opened in November of 2004. The roads were better than they had been when we first started out in 1998. Back then the roads had been so bumpy that all of our lights went out one night because a switch had jiggled loose. Our bikes fell off of the bike rack on the car the next day while we were being jostled around on the rough roads of Arkansas. We had road service to pay for the light problem, but the bike repairs were our own expense.

A highlight of that trip back to Maryland was visiting the Graceland Mansion again. We are big Elvis fans. Graceland had changed since we were there last. It had additions and we were glad we stopped. It was always a very emotional experience. Elvis was the only person ever to have been in the Rock and Roll Hall of Fame, the Country Music Hall of Fame, and the Gospel Music Hall of Fame. Besides that, he is in the Martial Arts Hall of Fame, an amazing human. Whether or not you are an Elvis fan, you would enjoy and marvel at those exhibits. We toured the National Ornamental

Metal Museum and the Southland Dog Races, also in Memphis. We had dinner on Beale Street and listened to blues music. Like Hollywood has famous names on its streets, Beale Street has notes on the sidewalks to immortalize many great musicians.

It took three days of driving to cross Tennessee, a wide state. We drove steadily until we reached Reisterstown, Maryland, stopping in Virginia one night to awaken to four inches of snow. There was also snow during the opening day Orioles baseball game in Baltimore. We were very lucky the day we arrived back at the condo in Reisterstown. We had just pulled into the driveway where we lived when the hitch on the car broke. After five years of full-time traveling, God had surely been good to us. We could have been traveling 60 miles per hour or on a dangerous road when that happened. We felt especially blessed to have been able to spend such an incredible five years on the road.

All the while we passed through Nevada, California, Arizona, New Mexico, Mexico, Texas, Arkansas, Tennessee, West Virginia, Virginia, and Maryland we had Flat Stanley with us. He was a project of a second grader in Illinois. A college friend sent Flat Stanley to us so that he could go on vacation with us and we could document his travels with post cards, souvenirs and pictures that we sent to the second grader at intervals. A teacher had started a project on the Internet, which had spread all over the country to other second graders. We met some other grandparents who also had Flat Stanley with them. It was a great way for students to learn more about geography and we were glad we could help. We liked dressing Flat Stanley in clothes, hats, and boots appropriate to the state we were passing through.

During our stay in Maryland, we were invited to a Habitat Dedication Ceremony in Baltimore where Millard Fuller, Habitat for Humanity's founder was speaking. It was good to have time to talk with him. That evening, we attended a dinner in Millard and Linda Fuller's honor, held at the Baltimore Raven's new stadium. After working for a couple of months in Maryland, we took the motor home to Warwick, New York for our youngest son's wedding on June 14th. Joshua and Christen went to Acadia National Park in Maine for their honeymoon and moved to Ipswich, Massachusetts in August. They met in the outdoors at LaVida wilderness camp, an outgrowth of Gordon College where they both graduated. The school had a graduation requirement that every student spend ten days in the wilderness, three of those days in solitude.

Joshua and Christen liked the program so much that they became camp counselors and got to know each other that way at LaVida.

Our plan after the wedding festivities was to tour all four of the Maritime Provinces of Eastern Canada, the only provinces of Canada that we had not been in before. Those are also referred to as the Atlantic Provinces and they included Nova Scotia, Newfoundland/Labrador, Prince Edward Island and New Brunswick. After leaving Warwick, we stopped in Hyde Park, New York to tour Franklin Delano Roosevelt's library and museum. Through this period of time, we had seen 11 of the 12 presidential libraries and meant we would have to make a trip out to Iowa to see President Herbert Hoover's library in the future.

As intended, we came through Maine and had lobster. We actually found it at the grocery store with a selection of fish displayed in abundance like we had never seen before. We drove through Skowhegan, Maine where we used to live. We met a bus driver who was transporting famous stars, Mel Gibson and Robin Williams in his own coach.

We visited Acadia National Park and then took a catamaran ferry, called the CAT from Bar Harbor, Maine to Nova Scotia in three hours. We had been allowed to stay the

night before in the ferry parking lot and it was a good thing because we tried to stay in the Visitors Center parking lot at Acadia National Park but just before ten o'clock, the ranger told us we couldn't stay there even though there were no signs posted. So we were right at the dock when it was time to get in line for the ferry at seven in the morning. The CAT is able to travel at 45 knots while carrying 1,000 passengers and 250 vehicles of varying sizes.

We had wonderfully warm days for our entire four-week trip. The scenery was much like Alaska. When we got to Nova Scotia, we stayed in Bridgewater and toured Lunenburg and Peggy's Cove in the car.

That turned out to be a very good decision because the motor home was having engine problems and while they fixed it, we toured. There is a memorial to lost sailors and ships in Lunenburg where we had a quaint lunch of mussels and haddock at the Magnolia Café. It wasn't right on the water but we enjoyed the food. The bumps or porch dormers on the old houses were pointed out to us as a peculiarity to that area. There were many lighthouses along the eastern coast of Nova Scotia as we drove along the unusually rugged landscape with huge rocks and unpredictable waves. We saw the site of the Flight #111 Memorial, where 229 passengers died in 1998. The lighthouse in Peggy's Cove was touted to be "the most photographed lighthouse on earth." Of course, we took pictures there!

We had to drive near Halifax to get to the West Coast of Nova Scotia but we didn't stop in Halifax. We did stop in Truro and walked into Victoria Park to see the triple Waddell Falls, a beautiful walk through the woods with wooden steps and railings. The mountains meeting the beaches were spectacular and we certainly were reminded of Scotland, at least as we would imagine Scotland. Our campground in Havre Boucher was on the water with a rocky beach instead of a sandy beach and we had a great view of a typical foggy morning. We crossed the Canso Causeway to get into Cape Breton Island, the northern part of Nova Scotia, where we toured the Alexander Graham Bell Museum in Baddeck. Part of his inventive nature took the form that it did because his wife was deaf and rich. They had come from Scotland to Ontario to Washington, DC and finally settled in Nova Scotia for his last 37 years. The Cabot Trail went around Cape Breton Island for 180 miles. All mileage in Canada was in kilometers, so we did a lot of transposing. They also used military time in Canada. There was an hour's difference in time from Maine to Nova Scotia and another one-half hour's difference just in Newfoundland! Cabot Trail took us through Cape Breton Highlands National Park and we saw lots of lobster traps piled up and down the roadways. We learned that the pink and purple flowers that lined the roads were called lupines. We didn't see many other types of blooms. We did see the Gulf of Saint Lawrence. All the water that we saw in the Maritime Provinces was so very deep blue and lovely. We traveled along the North River, the Little River, and the Ingonish River. We stopped in Saint Ann's at a church that also had a teahouse so the congregation could make extra money to keep the church running. We took a breathtaking picture at 902 feet on Cape Smokey Mountain overlooking the Atlantic Ocean. We stopped at Black Brook Cove and had a picnic lunch while watching the waves break on the rocks and we stopped at Wreck Cove Point, which was a whale-watching spot on the Gulf of Saint Lawrence. All the beaches we saw in those parts were rocky, not sandy.

We crossed the Bras d'Or Lake Bridge over Canada's inland sea and the Seal Island Bridge, spanning the part of the Bras d'Or Lake from Boularderie Island to Kelly's Mountain in Cape Breton to get fantastic views of the deep blue waters. We took the seven-hour ferry from North Sydney in Nova Scotia to Port Aux Basques in Newfoundland, called the Lief Erikson. The ferry was huge and was very expensive to ride, having to pay for two persons, a car and $10 per foot for the motor home! They even charged us for two extra feet because we carried bicycles on the back of our rig. We had to leave Baggins inside while we were required to leave the motor home. On that evening ferry, we saw one of many memorable sunsets that we would see throughout our visit to the Maritimes. We arrived at midnight and had a hard time trying to find our site in the dark provincial park, similar to the state parks in the United States. We spent all of our time in Newfoundland on the West Coast, traveling again on the Trans Canada Highway (Route 1), stopping in Corner Brook, the second largest city in Newfoundland, which doesn't say much for Saint John's on the eastern coast, which is the largest city. Corner Brook is at the mouth of the Humber River, one of the greatest salmon rivers in the world. We spent time at Gros Morne National Park and took several trail walks there where we got to see two beaver lodges close to our path around a pond. Gros Morne National Park is involved with geology and archeology for the United Nations. Although this is the area where the moose is the most populated in North America, it was not our fate to see any wildlife at all on that trip. We drove along the Viking Trail (Route 430), along the coast of the Gulf of Saint Lawrence, seeing rich views of blue water, rocks, and found a beach with sand, which seemed to be the exception in Newfoundland. We learned that Newfoundland's specialty was bakeapple pie, made from a berry called the bakeapple, but they were not in season so we couldn't try one. We saw a beautiful sunset from Rocky Harbour where the Bonne Bay and the Gulf of Saint Lawrence meet. We went back there another night for another sensational red sunset. On the way back to Port Aux Basques we stopped at the Discovery Center that is also a part of the national park. The same movies were shown there that they had at the Visitors Center, but those movies were on a big screen, so it would have been better to have seen them at the Discovery Center if we had known.

The same ferry ride back to Nova Scotia left at midnight and took 7-1/2 hours. That time, the ferry was called the Caribou. As we got onto the ferry, the border guards took our sweet potatoes out of our refrigerator because of a bad blight, even though we had brought them with us from the United States. Going the other way across the Canso Causeway, we again traveled to Havre Boucher, Nova Scotia. That was the world's deepest causeway, built in 1955 to prevent ice from entering the Strait of Canso from the north, allowing passage of oceangoing traffic the year round.

Next, we were headed to Prince Edward Island via another ferry, but the news program on television told us that the ferry could be on strike. Fortunately, it was not. So we took the Northumberland Ferries, Ltd. (NFL), called the Confederation to cross the Northumberland Strait into Prince Edward Island (PEI) and once again we were on the Trans Canada Highway. We were surprised to be greeted at the PEI Visitors Center with a huge provincial liquor store right next to it. Prices of liquor were very high in the Maritimes because of high taxes. There were also high taxes on cigarettes and gasoline, but not much else. A father of six told us that PEI was a great place to raise children. There were lots of farms, bigger houses than in Nova Scotia or Newfoundland/Labrador and there were just no problems that involved the children. The farms were all potato farms as PEI raised more potatoes than anywhere else in the world and that was all they grew. There were many varieties of potatoes. We stayed in a provincial park where the beaches were red sand and we had a perfect day for walking on the beach and rocks although the water was still too cold to do much swimming. We didn't have to pay for the ferry to get into PEI because the only tolls are paid when leaving the island. Before we left PEI, we drove to Chelton Beach with more red sand, although some of the PEI beaches are white. The differences were interesting to see. We left via the nine-mile Confederation Bridge from Borden-Carleton across the Northumberland Strait again, into Cape Jourimain, New Brunswick. There we did pay the toll but it was not as expensive as the ferry toll would have been had we left that way.

The government must figure it all works itself out so they are not losing tourist money that is very important to them. One of the most visited tourist spots in PEI was Anne of Green Gables but we did not go that far out of our way, as time was not as available as we might have liked.

We traveled on the eastern coast of New Brunswick beside the Bay of Fundy where there are the highest tides in the world. At Hopewell Rocks the tides become 36 feet to as high as 50 feet in a 12-hour period. It was an awesome sight to have viewed the beaches during the low tides when one could walk on them and then again view the beaches at high tide when they were covered. We went kayaking with a group in Fundy National Park when the tides were high. What accounts for such high tides is due in part to the normal high tides of that area in addition to the swooshing back and forth in a narrow body of water. The Bay of Fundy sits between the provinces of Nova Scotia and New Brunswick. When we got to Saint John in New Brunswick (not to be confused with Saint John's in Newfoundland), we had dinner in a restaurant overlooking the Reversing Falls, another phenomenon of New Brunswick. That is where the Bay of Fundy meets the 450-mile-long Saint John River and causes the river waters to be pushed backward. That unique phenomenon of the Reversing Falls is caused by the tremendous rise and fall of the tides of the Bay of Fundy, which make the Saint John River change direction. At  low tide the water in the Bay of Fundy is 14 feet lower than the natural level of the Saint John River. The river plunges over cascading falls and has to yield to the superior power of the Bay of Fundy. At high tide the tides actually rise higher than the river level and forces the river to flow upstream, even to the point of causing uphill rapids in the river.

In the center of town we walked around fountains and gardens where there were memorials to the Great War I and the Great War II, as they are called in Canada, as well as the Old City Market, where we bought lobster rolls which we found out were similar to our seafood-salad subs. We had seen advertisements for them throughout the Maritime Provinces and were curious. We drove through the Irving Nature Trail Park on the Bay of Fundy and walked Baggins along the water's edge. In Saint Andrew's, further down the coast of New Brunswick, we visited the 1824 Presbyterian Church and the Kingsbrae Gardens as well as the oldest practicing church in all of Canada, another Presbyterian church dating back to 1790. Having continued down the coast, the highlight of our trip may have been in Saint George when we got to see the salmon swimming against the current, going to spawn. It was very exciting! The engineers had made a group of steps, called ladders, so that the salmon could climb and have a place to rest. Because of a dam that had been built which kept the salmon from their natural route, there was a huge drop creating a waterfall that the salmon just couldn't fight. It was fascinating to see them climbing against the current step-by-step, pausing to rest. It was very near the end of the spawning season, so we were fortunate to be there in time to see that. New Brunswick turned out to be our favorite of the Maritimes.

On our way out of New Brunswick in the border town of Saint Stephen, we celebrated Canada Day, which is July first, in the courtyard of the town on the Saint Croix River, with music and a decadent chocolate dessert. Saint Stephen is known for its chocolates and we did not want to miss out. We crossed over into Calais, Maine where the border guards took our frozen lamb patties out of our freezer because of mad cow disease. We were surprised when both border guards in Canada and in the United States boarded the motor home and looked into our refrigerator and freezer. With all the compartments we have inside and outside of the motor home, that was the only place they looked.

As soon as we crossed the border from Maine into the Province of Quebec, on the Highway of President Kennedy, all the signs were in French only. The roads were not good but we thoroughly enjoyed visiting Old Quebec City on the Saint Lawrence River. We arrived there just as the Quebec Festival was beginning. The Old City was surrounded by huge stone walls with arches at the many entrances built long ago for protection. We were entranced by the city. It seemed like places in Europe would be. We lunched in a French Bistro on Saint Jean Street (Ste. Jean St.) and visited the

Cathedral of Notre-Dame. We had a strange experience parking the car in a garage. There were no attendants and we found a booth that looked like a phone booth in the middle of the garage with instructions in French about where to park the car. We figured out how to pay with a credit card and to leave the ticket we purchased on the dashboard of the car so that they would know we had paid for our parking. One evening, we had a business dinner with four men: Yves, Pierre, Michelle, and Jerome, the heads of a company that Bob had been dealing with at work. First there were bottles of white wine, then bottles of red wine. Fortunately the men all spoke English although with heavy accents. Another day, we went into the lower part of Old Quebec City, so very charming with cobblestone roads, shops and outdoor restaurants with seating up and down the hills, with bright colors, street performers, lots of steps in order to view the Saint Lawrence River from the Dufferin Terrace, and a boardwalk off the immense hotel, Chateau Frontenac. We drove back to the campground in Pont-Rouge via Champlain Rue along the Saint Lawrence River and under the bridges, an extraordinary view and our favorite part of the Province of Quebec, perhaps of all of Canada. Quebec City was so enchanting and quaint. We learned about something that seemed very strange to us. Moving Day in Quebec City was the first day of July for everybody who rented. Most of the tenants wanted to move somewhere else and everybody must move on that day. We saw furniture piled high everywhere and moving trucks backing into apartments, tying up traffic. To us it seemed a very odd system. To the residents there, it seemed very normal and expected.

At the United States border, again in Maine, they wanted to take our meat and fruit but that time they didn't enter the motor home so we didn't have to give up anything. We traveled through Maine, Vermont, and New Hampshire to get to Wenham, Massachusetts to visit our son and his new wife. We attended a game at the Boston Red Sox Fenway Park. They were playing against the Baltimore Orioles and we had great bleacher seats in the oldest park in major league baseball. After a Connecticut visit with Bob's cousin, we tried to get into the New York Mets Shea Stadium, but we had to be satisfied with taking pictures outside as we did not arrive in time to get into the game. We got caught up in traffic in an effort to see Ground Zero. As we passed by, there was not much to see as it was all walled off. We were able to get tickets to the New York

Yankees baseball game at Yankee Stadium in the Bronx. That was an evening we really enjoyed.

We camped in a New Jersey campground for two weeks. Besides seeing our children and some friends, I had the opportunity to keep a 10-year-old Fresh Air child from New York City. We had been part of the Fresh Air Fund for many years. It was a wonderful free program for disadvantaged children from New York City to get to spend two weeks with a host family in a country setting. For many it was the only vacation the child would ever get and it gave the children a chance to see how other people lived. Several states in the New York City area participated. We had previously hosted children in New Jersey and Maryland and had also been part of the screening process and on the team to escort the children on the bus trip from New York City to their host families in neighboring states.

After getting back to work in Reisterstown for the rest of the summer and fall, we were faced with the bad Hurricane Isabelle which blew out the transformers in our area. As we were going to be without electricity anyway, we got in the motor home and took a short trip to Pennsylvania where we met up with our son, John to see a Philadelphia Phillies game at Veterans Stadium. It was the last year that old stadium would be used. It was to be imploded in March, 2004. We enjoyed a nice evening out and when we returned to Reisterstown, our electricity had been returned and we went to a favorite Mexican restaurant to celebrate my birthday.

Although Maryland was experiencing record high temperatures, we left in early November for a trip to Florida. Our first night out was spent near Deswell, Virginia in a Flying J truck stop where there were many motor homes and fifth-wheel trailers camping there for the night. We had not seen a separate place for RVers any other time we had stopped at a truck stop, so that was a nice occurrence. Previously, we had trouble with our carbon-monoxide detector going off in the middle of the night because of truck fumes. The more we were on the road, the more we learned. And that night we saw our first lunar eclipse.

We went through Hilton Head, South Carolina again and camped in Saint Augustine, Florida where we had not been before. Friends there took us on a tour of the city and the Atlantic Ocean beach at night. After a stop in Ocala and one in Lakeland, we stayed at a city park in Florida City so we could see nearby Biscayne National Park. In the canal there, we saw two manatees feeding near the shore. Manatees are very sweet aquatic mammals with broad, rounded tails, sometimes referred to as sea cows. Some weigh over 3,000 pounds. They are indigenous to that part of the country.

Our goal for going to Florida was to see the Dry Tortugas National Park. In order to do that, we had to travel through the Florida Keys which was a delightful experience. All the way down Route 1 were spectacular green waters on both sides. The Spanish word for island is Che, which Americans changed to Key, so instead of those string of islands being called islands, they are called Keys. Manatee mailboxes and manatee souvenirs of all sorts were everywhere. We could not forget that we were in manatee country. Bridge after bridge after bridge, about 20 of them, took us from one Key to the other. We drove on the Seven-Mile Bridge that was the longest causeway in the Keys over the Moser Channel. Part of Route 1 was very dangerous with no passing zones for long stretches at a time. Signs read: "Patience Please - Three Miles to Passing Zone."

When we got to Key West, the southern most point of the United States, we were thrilled to see kite boarders. We had to ask what they were called. The rider was between what looked like a big skateboard and a parachute, holding onto the strings to make it go in the direction he wanted. They would rise up above the water in what looked like a very exhilarating experience. Utilizing the wonderful weather, we walked along beaches, docks and around the campground that was on the Gulf of Mexico. The water seemed just a bit too cool for swimming but sunbathing was great. In the evening, we went to Mallory Square where there were innumerable street performers offering more energized presentations along the boardwalk than on the traditional stage. Assuredly, wherever cruise ships docked, you could count on seeing unusual live enter-tainment not available on late night entertainment TV. We saw dogs performing tricks. A man did 25 push-ups with his legs straight up into the air. An escape artist from the Houdini Hall of Fame also performed. There were too many performers lined up and down the boardwalks for us to see them all. In the town itself was the famous Duvall Street that seemed much like the streets of New Orleans, Louisiana, although drinks were not allowed on the sidewalks and streets.

On the afternoon that we were supposed to take a seaplane out to Dry Tortugas National Park, 68 miles away in the Gulf of Mexico, the wind kicked up to 33 knots and the trip was cancelled. That posed a problem since we only planned to stay at the campground for two nights. Instead of paying our usual six dollars a night for a Coast to Coast campground, that private one was costing us $60 a night. Being able to book an early morning seaplane the next day, the campground host allowed us to stay until two the next afternoon, meaning that we wouldn't have to pay the extra night. We were grateful we had chosen to go to the Dry Tortugas by seaplane instead of by boat. It cost a little more but almost all of the people who went by boat got very sick. The same winds, although not as strong, that had kept us from taking the trip the day before made the boat ride very rocky. I do get seasick, so I was extremely thankful for our choice. The seaplane excursion allowed for us to have snorkeling equipment, so when we landed on the beach at the Dry Tortugas we headed for the water to try out our snorkeling skills. It has been a very long time since we had tried that sport. Unfortunately due to the storm the day before, the water was very cloudy and rough and we could not see any fish. The water was cold and the high waves made it impossible for us to go very far from the shore. Under normal conditions the waters are a light blue in color with coral reefs close enough to see spectacular scenery and fish. Instead, we changed back into our warmer clothing and enjoyed touring the fort that was the only structure on the island. Dry Tortugas National Park was originally named Tortugas National Park because tortugas in Spanish means turtles and many turtles of great proportion inhabited those waters. Later when it was realized no fresh water, only salt water was available on the island, the name was altered to include that idea, making it the Dry Tortugas. There were about 12 employees of the National Park Service who lived permanently on the island. Once a month they used a supply boat to get into Key West. Each employee or couple had their own apartment right inside the old fort. The employees collected rainwater and also used the reverse osmosis process to turn salt water into usable drinking water. One couple had been there for three years as part of their stint with the National Park Service, an interesting choice for a newly married young couple.

Fort Jefferson was built in the 1800s to keep food and other supplies that were coming from New Orleans around the tip of the Florida Keys to the East Coast of the

United States safe from pirates and unfriendly countries. The fort's weaponry was outdated before the structure was ever completed. We were able to walk around the entire fort as well as climb to the top for an extraordinary view of the Gulf of Mexico and the other islands that were part of the Dry Tortugas National Park. They, however, had nothing on them and were really too small to even stop for. The excursion back to Key West in the seaplane had amazing scenery. We could see clear water, coral reefs, many small islands, some with houses, and many birds. Seeing that national park meant that we had seen 46 of the 55 national parks on our list. We probably would never see the four in Alaska that can only be reached by plane. We had yet to see Black Canyon of the Gunnison in Colorado, Haleakala in Hawaii, Isle Royale in Michigan, Cuyahoga Valley in Ohio, or the Virgin Islands in Saint Thomas.

On our way further north into the Florida mainland we stopped in Miami to see the Pro Player Stadium where the Florida Marlins played major league baseball. As mentioned before, some stadiums allowed anyone to wander about inside and outside, some allowed tours and some only allowed spectators in to see a game. That was one in which we could not go inside because it was not baseball season, so we had to limit our pictures to outside shots. With that stadium, we had seen 27 of the 30 major league parks and some of them we had seen an old stadium and a new one. We still needed to get to the Minnesota Twins Metrodome, the Cincinnati Reds' Great American Ballpark, the Milwaukee Brewers' Miller Park and the brand new 2004 stadiums for the Chicago White Sox, the Philadelphia Phillies, and the San Diego Padres.

We found a beautifully wooded campground at Rock Crusher RV Resort in Crystal River, Florida that coincidentally was the same city in Florida where we had bought our first motor home. We thoroughly enjoyed the Thanksgiving and Christmas holidays. In Crystal River, we learned about the whooping crane relocation program. On December eighth, 16 whooping cranes led by ultra light planes with pilots disguised as whooping cranes arrived from the Necedah National Wildlife Refuge in Central Wisconsin. They had left there on October 16th, headed for Chassahowitzka National Wildlife Refuge in Southwest Citrus County, Florida. Their progress had been followed and hundreds of people gathered at the north end of the Crystal River Mall to greet the birds as they flew over to their winter home. Those birds were being taught a new migration route and trained by humans to make Florida their winter home in an effort to make certain that whooping cranes, the tallest and most famous endangered North American bird, did not become extinct. In the 1940s the population was down to 15 birds. That flock in the late 1990s, consisting of about 180 birds, was the only naturally occurring wild population of whooping cranes in the world. That was when the Americans and the Canadians got together to try to save them. We found it neat that we had stayed in both areas of the United States where whooping cranes migrate - from Wisconsin to Citrus County, Florida, with help of relocators, and from Northern Wood Buffalo National Park which borders Alberta and the Northwest Territories in Canada to Aransas National Wildlife Refuge in Rockport, Texas, by nature.

The campground we chose, Rock Crusher RV Resort, was very different from most campgrounds in which we had previously spent time. The site was huge with plenty of roaming room for Baggins. He loved to lie outside and bask in the sun or the shade, both having been amply provided. We enjoyed the quiet and peacefulness, more like state and provincial parks than most campground resorts. The campers were friendly and the wooded areas that surrounded the outdoor heated pool and spa added to the serenity. It was a spot we would remember in the future as we thought about the end of the year 2003 and the many wonderful trips we had experienced on our journey since 1997.

Author's Note

Travels With Charlie written in 1962 by John Steinbeck talked about integration in the United States during that time. And at that time, I, too, would have wanted to talk about integration. Thankfully, during the time that Mr. Steinbeck was on the road, we were in high schools that were integrated.

We are happy to report that in the time of our travels from 1997 until 2003, we didn't run into the sort of racial problems that existed in the 1960s.

APPENDIX A

National Parks Alphabetically by Name

Name of National Park(55)	City & State	Abbreviation	Date There
1 Acadia	Bar Harbor, Maine	ME	06-16-03
2 Arches	Moab, Utah	UT	03-25-01
3 Badlands	Interior, South Dakota	SD	08-10-98
4 Big Bend	Big Bend, Texas	TX	03-14-01
5 Biscayne	Homestead, Florida	FL	11-17-03
6 Black Canyon of the Gunnison	Gunnison, Colorado	CO	
7 Bryce Canyon	Bryce Canyon, Utah	UT	03-28-01
8 Canyonlands	Moab, Utah	UT	03-25-01
9 Capital Reef	Torrey, Utah	UT	03-27-01
10 Carlsbad Caverns	Carlsbad, New Mexico	NM	05-27-98
11 Channel Islands	Ventura, California	CA	01-03-03
12 Crater Lake	Crater Lake, Oregon	OR	09-29-99
13 Cuyahoga Valley	Brecksville, Ohio	OH	
14 Death Valley	Death Valley, California	CA/NV	03-08-98
15 Denali	Park, Alaska	AK	06-01-01
16 Dry Tortugas	Homestead, Florida	FL	11-20-03
17 Everglades	Homestead, Florida	FL	03-09-99
18 Gates of the Artic	Fairbanks, Alaska	AK	05-29-01
			Visitors Center Only
19 Glacier Bay	Gustavus, Alaska	AK	No Roads
20 Glacier	West Glacier, Montana	MT	09-16-99
21 Grand Canyon	Grand Canyon, Arizona	AZ	05-23-98
22 Grand Tetons	Moose, Wyoming	WY	09-15-99
23 Great Basin	Baker, Nevada	NV	05-06-01
24 Great Smoky Mountain	Gatlinburg, TN/NC	TN	11/15/98
25 Guadalupe Mountain	Salt Flat, Texas	TX	05-30-98
26 Haleakala	Makawao, Hawaii	HI	
27 Hawaii Volcanoe	Hawaii National Park, Hawaii	HI	02-15-89
28 Hot Springs	Hot Springs, Arkansas	AR	12-12-01
29 Isle Royale	Houghton, Michigan	MI	

Name of National Park(55)	City & State	Abbreviation	Date There
30 Joshua Tree	Twentynine Palms, California	CA	03-31-98
31 Katmai	King Salmon, Alaska	AK	NoRoads
32 Kenai Fjords	Seward, Alaska	AK	06-28-01
33 Kings Canyon	Three Rivers, California	CA	10-07-99
34 Kobuk Valley	Kotzebue, Alaska	AK	No Roads
35 Lake Clark	Anchorage, Alaska	AK	No Roads
36 Lassen Volcanic	Mineral, California	CA	10-03-99
37 Mammoth Cave	Mammoth Cave, Kentucky	KY	11-10-98
38 Mesa Verde	Mesa Verde, Colorado	CO	03-25-01
39 Mount Rainier	Ashford, Washington	WA	09-26-99
40 North Cascades	Sedro Woolley, Washington	WA	09-23-99
41 Olympic	Port Angeles, Washington	WA	09-27-99
42 Petrified Forest	Petrified Forest N P, Arizona	AZ	05-24-98
43 Redwood	Crescent City, California	CA	10-02-99
44 Rocky Mountain	Estes Park, Colorado	CO	03-19-01
45 Saguaro	Tucson, Arizona	AZ	03-11-03
46 Sequoia	Three Rivers, California	CA	10-07-99
47 Shenandoah	Luray, Virginia	VA	05-31-99
48 Theodore Roosevelt	Medora, North Dakota	ND	09-14-99
49 Virgin Islands	St. Thomas, Virgin Islands	VI	
50 Voyageurs	International Falls, Minnesota	MN	09-11-99
51 Wind Cave	Hot Springs, South Dakota	SD	08-12-98
52 Wrangell-St. Elias	Glennallen, Alaska	AK	07-17-01
53 Yellowstone	Yellowstone N P, Wyoming	WY/MT/ID	09-13-99
54 Yosemite	Yosemite N P, California	CA	10-06-99
55 Zion	Springdale, Utah	UT	03-28-01

APPENDIX B

National Parks Alphabetically by State

Alaska AK
Denali
Gates of the Artic [1]
Glacier Bay [2]
Katmai [2]
Kenai Fjords
Kobuk Valley [2]
Lake Clark [2]
Wrangell - St. Elias

Arizona AZ
Grand Canyon
Petrified Forest
Saguaro

Arkansas AR
Hot Springs

California CA
Channel Islands
Death Valley
Joshua Tree
Kings Canyon
Lassen Volcanic
Redwood
Sequoia
Yosemite

Colorado CO
Black Canyon of the Gunnison
Mesa Verde
Rocky Mountain

Florida FL
Biscayne
Dry Tortugas
Everglades

Hawaii HI
Haleakala
Hawaii

Kentucky KY
Mammoth Cave

Maine ME
Acadia

Michigan MI
Isle Royale

Minnesota MN
Voyageurs

Montana MT
Glacier

Nevada NV
Great Basin

New Mexico NM
Carlsbad Caverns

New Dakota ND
Theodore Roosevelt

Ohio OH
Cuyahoga Valley

[1] Visitor Center only
[2] By Plane only

Oregon OR
Crater Lake

South Dakota SD
Badlands
Wind Cave

Tennessee TN
Great Smoky Mountains

Texas TX
Big Bend
Guadalupe Mountains

Utah UT
Arches
Bryce Canyon
Canyonlands
Capital Reef
Zion

Virgin Islands VI
Virgin Islands

Virginia VA
Shenandoah

Washington WA
Mount Rainier
North Cascades
Olympic

Wyoming WY
Grand Teton
Yellowstone

APPENDIX C

Major League Ball Parks Alphabetically by City or State in Each League

Name of Team	Name of Park	Year Park Was Built
	AMERICAN LEAGUE	
1 Anaheim Angels	Los Angeles Wrigley Field	1961
	Dodger Stadium	1962
	Anaheim Stadium	1966
	Edison International Field, renovated and renamed in	1997
	Angel Stadium, renamed	2004
2 Baltimore Orioles	Lloyd Street Grounds	1901
	Sportsman's Park	1902
	Memorial Stadium	1954
	Oriole Park at Camden Yards	1992
3 Boston Red Sox	Huntington Avenue Grounds	1901
	Fenway Park	1912
4 Chicago White Sox	South Side Park	1901
	Comiskey Park	1910
	Comiskey Park II	1991
	U.S. Cellular Field, renamed in	2003
	renovated in	2004
5 Cleveland Indians	League Park	1901
	Cleveland Stadium	1932
	Jacobs Field	1994
6 Detroit Tigers	Bennett Park	1901
	Navin Field	1912
	Briggs Stadium	1937
	Tiger Stadium, renamed in	1961
	renovated in	1993
	Comerica Park	2000
7 Kansas City Royals	Municipal Stadium	1969
	Royals Stadium	1973
	Kauffman Stadium, renamed in	1993
	renovated in	1999
8 Minnesota Twins	American League Park	1901
	Griffith Stadium	1911
	Metropolitan Stadium	1961
	Hubert H. Humphrey Metrodome	1982
9 New York Yankees	American League Park	1901
	Hilltop Park	1903
	Polo Grounds	1913
	Yankee Stadium	1923
	Shea Stadium	1974
	Yankee Stadium	1976
10 Oakland Athletics	Columbia Park	1901

Name of Team	Name of Park	Year Park Was Built
AMERICAN LEAGUE		
10 Oakland Athletics (Con't.)	Shibe Park	1909
	Municipal Stadium	1955
	Oakland-Alameda County Coliseum	1968
	Network Associates Coliseum, renamed about	1973
	renovated in	2001
11 Seattle Mariners	Kingdome	1977
	Safeco Field	1999
12 Tampa Bay Devil Rays	Tropicana Park	1998
13 Texas Rangers	Griffith Stadium	1961
	Robert F. Kennedy Stadium	1962
	Arlington Stadium	1972
	The Ballpark in Arlington	1994
14 Toronto Blue Jays	Exhibition Stadium	1977
	Skydome	1989
NATIONAL LEAGUE		
1 Arizona Diamondbacks	Bank One Ballpark	1998
2 Atlanta Braves	South End Grounds	1874
	Braves Field	1914
	County Stadium	1953
	Atlanta-Fulton County Stadium	1966
	Turner Field	1997
3 Chicago Cubs	State Street Grounds	1876
	Lakefront Park	1878
	Westside Park	1885
	Brotherhood Park	1891
	West Side Grounds	1893
	Weeghman Park	1916
	Cubs Park	1920
	Wrigley Field	1926
4 Cincinnati Reds	Lincoln Park Grounds	1876
	Avenue Grounds	1876
	Bank Street Grounds	1880
	League Park	1890
	Palace of the Fans	1902
	Crosley Field	1912
	Riverfront Stadium	1970
	Cinergy Field, renamed in	1997
	Great American Ballpark	2003
5 Colorado Rockies	Mile High Stadium (used for football when built)	1993
	Coors Field	1995
6 Florida Marlins	Joe Robbie Stadium	1993
	Pro Player Stadium, renamed in	1997

Name of Team	Name of Park	Year Park Was Built
	NATIONAL LEAGUE	
7 Houston Astros	Colt Stadium	1962
	Astrodome	1965
	Enron Field	2000
	Minute Maid Park, renamed in	2002
8 Los Angeles Dodgers	Washington park	1890
	Ebbets Field	1913
	Memorial Coliseum	1958
	Dodger Stadium	1962
9 Milwaukee Brewers	Sicks Stadium	1969
	County Stadium	1970
	Miller Park	2001
10 Montreal Expos	Jarry Park	1969
	Stade Olympique	1977
11 New York Mets	Polo Grounds	1962
	Shea Stadium	1964
12 Philadelphia Phillies	Philadelphia Base Ball Grounds	1887
	Baker Bowl	1895
	Connie Mack Stadium	1953
	Veterans Stadium	1971
	Citizens Bank Park	2004
13 Pittsburgh Pirates	Exposition Park	1891
	Forbes Field	1909
	Three Rivers Stadium	1970
	PNC Park (on same site)	2001
14 Saint. Louis Cardinals	Robinson Field	1893
	Sportsman's Park	1920
	Busch Stadium,	1966
	renovated in	1997
15 San Diego Padres	Jack Murphy Stadium	1969
	Qualcomm Stadium, renamed in	1997
	Petco Park	2004
16 San Francisco Giants	Polo Grounds (1)	1883
	Oakland Park	1889
	St. George Grounds	1889
	Polo Grounds (2)	1889
	Polo Grounds (3)	1891
	Seals Stadium	1958
	Candlestick Park	1960
	3Com Park, renamed in	1996
	Pacific Bell Park	2000
	SBC Park, renamed in	2004

APPENDIX D

Presidential Libraries Alphabetically by Last Name

1. George Bush Library
1000 George Bush Drive West
College Station, TX 77845

2. Jimmy Carter Library
441 Freedom Parkway
Atlanta, GA 30307-1498

3. Clinton Presidential Materials Project
1000 LaHarpe Boulevard
Little Rock, AR 72201

4. Dwight D. Eisenhower Library
200 SE 4th Street
Abilene, KS 67410-2900

5. Gerald R. Ford Library
1000 Beal Avenue
Ann Arbor, MI 48109-2114

6. Herbert Hoover Library
210 Parkside Drive
West Branch, IA 52358-0488

7. Lyndon B. Johnson Library
2313 Red River Street
Austin, TX 78705-5702

8. John F. Kennedy Library
Columbia Point
Boston, MA 02125-3398

9. Richard Nixon Library & Birthplace
18001 Yorba Linda Boulevard
Yorba Linda, CA 92886-3949

10. Ronald Reagan Library
40 Presidential Drive
Simi Valley, CA 93065-0600

11. Franklin D. Roosevelt Library
4079 Albany Post Road
Hyde Park, NY 12538-1999

12. Harry S. Truman Library
500 West U.S. Highway 24
Independence, MO 64050-1798

APPENDIX E

Doggie Friendly Campgrounds Alphabetically by Province, Territory, or State

CANADA

MacLean Rotary Park
PO Box 6306
Ft. St. John, British Columbia, Canada
V1J4H8
250-785-1700
Trail around lake in park

Rest Area on Route #1 near Swift Current
Saskatchewan, Canada
Room to roam

Sportsman's Overnight Camping
Dry Pine Bay Road
Alban, Ontario Canada POM1AO
705-857-0461
Daqust Lake Road

Suspension Bridge
Whitehorse, Yukon Territory
Yukon River path

UNITED STATES

Gilbert Ray Campground
McCain Loop Drive
Tucson Mountain Park, Arizona 85735
520-883-4200
Along the river bed

Santa Fe Park
5707 Santa Fe Street
San Diego, California 92109
800-959-3787
Fenced in long dog run, unleashed
Ocean doggie beach nearby

McGrath State Beach Campground
2211 Harbor Blvd.
Oxnard, California 93030
805-968-1033
Beach dunes

Blanca RV Park
521 Main Street
Blanca, Colorado 81123
719-379-3201
Field just outside the park

Mojave River Fork Campground
Highway 38, San Bernardino National Forest
Redlands, California 92373
909-383-5588

Colorado Heights Camping Resort
19575 Monument Hill Road
Monument, Colorado 80132
719-481-2336
Field behind the back fence

Trinidad Lake State Park
Route 25
Trinidad, Colorado 81082
806-678-2267
Man-made lake

Lake Williams Campground
1742 Exeter Road, Route 207
Lebanon, Connecticut 06249
860-642-7761
Through the woods along the lake

Rock Crusher Canyon
275 S. Rock Crusher Road
Crystal River, Florida 34429
352-795-1313
Behind site #127, a hedge,
         fenced running spot

Country Lakes Campground
1877 Hickory Head Road
Quitman, Georgia 31643
229-263-5350
Room to roam

Cottonwood Camping
115 S. 130th
Bonner Springs, Kansas 66012
913-422-8038
Trail in woods across the road

Abita Springs Campground
24150 Highway 435
Abita Springs, Louisiana 70420
985-892-3565
Around the pond

Wagon Wheel Campground
27 Ocean Park Road
Old Orchard Beach, Maine 04064
207-934-4477
Woods beside the brook

Gitchee Gummee RV Park
2048M-28 East
Marquette, Michigan 49855
906-249-9102
Across the road from Lake Superior's beach

Preferred RV Park
1801 Crawford Way
Pahrump, Nevada 89048
800-445-7840
Desert across the road from park entrance

Outdoor World Lake and Shore Campground
545 Corson Tavern Road
Ocean View, New Jersey 08230
609-624-1494
Path around the lake

Pancho Villa State Park
PO Box 224
Columbus, New Mexico 88029
505-531-2711
Field at the back of the campground

Valley of the Fires, Bureau of Land Management
PO Box 871
Carrizozo, New Mexico 88301
505-648-2241
Malpais Native Trail through lava rocks

UNITED STATES

Four Bears Casino Park
202 Frontage Road
New Town, North Dakota 58763
800-294-5454
On the Missouri River

RV Park Turtle River State Park
3084 Park Avenue
Arvilla, North Dakota 58214
800-807-4723
Agassiz Campground

Baileyton Inn Campground
7485 Horton Highway
Baileyton, Tennessee 37745
423-234-4992
Big open fields

Timberline Campground
1204 Murfreesboro Road
Lebanon, Tennessee 37090
615-449-2831
Room to roam at the end of the park

Lake of the Woods
17446 Pintail Drive
Flint, Texas 75762
903-825-7755
Woods around the lake

Big Bend Travel Park
Highway 118 at Route 170
Terlingua, Texas 79852
432-371-2218
Along the river bed of Terlingua Creek

Lake Conroe Thousand Trails
11720 Old Montgomery Road
Willis, Texas 77318
800-807-6097
Around the lake

Big Bear Lake Camplands
Route 3, Box 204
Bruceton Mills, West Virginia 26525
304-379-4382
Room to roam

Rock Ridge Resort
17 Rock Ridge Drive
Pipestem, West Virginia 25979
304-466-0900
Path between trees, near site #48

APPENDIX F

Highly Recommended Places to Visit Alphabetically by Province and State

CANADA

Saint George's spawning salmon
New Brunswick Province

Old Quebec City
Quebec Province

UNITED STATES

Kenai Peninsula
Soldotna, AK

Bellagio's Casino
Las Vegas, NV

Grand Canyon National Park
Grand Canyon, AZ

Hoover Dam
Near Boulder City, NV

Dodgers Stadium
Los Angeles, CA

Turner Falls Park
Davis, OK

Forest Lawn Cemetery
Glendale, CA

Crater Lake National Park
Crater Lake, OR

Redwoods National Park
Orick, CA

Graceland
Memphis, TN

Lincoln and Viet Nam Memorials
Springfield, IL

Lyndon Baines Johnson Library
Austin, TX

Precious Moments Chapel
Carthage, MO

National Parks
Southern Utah

North Cascade National Park, Route 20
Sedro Woolley, WA

APPENDIX G

Other Items of Possible Interest to the Reader

RV Repair and Maintenance Manual edited by Bob Livingston
Published by Trailer Life Books
PO Box 4500, Agoura, CA 91301

Full-time RVing: A Complete Guide to Life on the Open Road
by Bill and Jan Moeller

The Theology of the Hammer by Millard Fuller

More Than Houses by Millard Fuller

A Simple, Decent Place to Live by Millard Fuller

I-800-HABITAT or
www.habitat.org

Coast to Coast Resorts
www.coastresorts.com

FMCA (Family Motor Coach Association)
1-800-543-3622 or www.fmca.com

Good Sam Club
www.goodsamclub.com